CITIZENS IN
ACTION
A GUIDE TO INFLUENCING GOVERNMENT

Columbia Books & Information Services – Bethesda, Maryland

ACKNOWLEDGEMENTS

This book would never have been possible without years and years (and years, yes, I'm old) of experience with some of the most dedicated public servants on the planet. In particular, I have learned, and continue to learn, a great deal from former U.S. House Representative Mike Kreidler (D-WA) and current U.S. House Representative Earl Blumenauer (D-OR), as well as the many talented individuals working with them.

Many other professionals participated in the development of this book, from nonprofit executives to citizen activists to, yes, even lobbyists. I showed up in Washington, D.C. in the late 1980's absolutely sure that I had all the answers. I had, after all, just completed my Bachelor's Degree in Political Science. To those who put up with me in my early years and are still talking to me now, I salute you.

It has been my honor since those early years to regularly harass (some might say "consult with") a wide range of truly committed advocacy professionals whose comments and insights have been invaluable. My colleagues at Advocacy Associates, LLC have likewise been inexpressibly helpful, not just in reviewing drafts, but in giving me the time and space needed to get the manuscript done and delivered, somewhat on time, to the publisher. And speaking of the publishers, Columbia Books and its fabulous staff, including Christy Talbot, my editor, and Joel Poznansky, the head honcho, must be commended (or condemned) for taking a chance on a publication that many other publishers said "wouldn't sell." Let's prove those other publishers wrong, shall we?

Finally, of course, nothing is possible without the family who supports you and understands why you must, yet again, sit at the computer to write instead of doing something more fun and less painful, like going to the dentist. My very patient husband Tim Silva deserves a lot of credit for what you're about to read.

The most important person here, though, is you – the committed and about to be amazingly effective citizen advocate. Thank you for reading this book. Now, onward – and happy advocating!

Stephanie Vance

TABLE OF CONTENTS

Title	Page

How many times have you thought "hey, there ought to be a law about that?" Whether it's "there ought to be a stop light there," "there ought to be laws that protect my children from unsafe drivers," or "there ought to be changes to the tax laws that save me money," the only way these goals will be achieved is through advocacy.

✪ What is Advocacy?

What is advocacy? I'm glad you asked. Look in any dictionary and you'll find a definition along these lines: Advocacy is "the act of pleading or arguing in favor of something, such as a cause, idea, or policy; active support." (American Heritage Dictionary). But that leaves things pretty wide-open, doesn't it? Under this definition, your efforts to get your kids to clean their rooms could be considered advocacy. Heck, I've even advocated at my dog (as in, "I'm pleading with you: please don't eat my favorite pumps.")

Technically speaking, there are many types of advocacy, ranging from trying to convince a judge that your client is innocent (legal advocacy), trying to persuade a school to help your special needs child (child advocacy) or taking on the increasingly complex and often overwhelming task of getting adequate and affordable medical care (patient advocacy). In each of these circumstances one person (a lawyer, parent or patient advocate, in these cases) pleads or argues in favor of a particular cause, idea or individual. For myself, I am a huge fan of "spousal advocacy," or the fine art of convincing your spouse to run the dishwasher every once in a while.

This book focuses on policy or legislative advocacy, which we'll define as the effort to convince others to agree with you on a particular policy idea. In general, those "others" are elected officials, because they are the ones most likely to make a decision about the policy idea you favor. However, in some cases your audience might be regulators, local opinion leaders or even fellow citizens. We'll discuss each of these different types of audiences throughout the book.

✪ What Isn't Advocacy?

Now, some may think of advocacy in this context as just another fancy word for "lobbying." Yuck. Aren't those the people that get paid hundreds of dollars an hour to bribe politicians on behalf of clients they really don't care all that much about? Except for the hundreds of dollars an hour part, no one wants to be a lobbyist, do they?

Wait, wait. Before you put this book down, let me assure you this is not a book about "influence peddling." It's not about pleading on behalf of causes you might not care that much about in exchange for cold, hard cash. Don't misinterpret: lobbying is actually a perfectly respectable and, in many cases, downright noble profession. In fact, your association or corporation likely has lobbyists in Washington, D.C. or at a state capitol who lobby on behalf of your cause. What sets the noble lobbyist apart from the, well, not-so-noble is a personal belief in the idea being advocated. In a word, it's authenticity.

✪ Why Advocate?

So you've worked with your association or corporation to identify an issue about which you care strongly. You're even convinced that some sort of governmental action (or change in existing actions) would improve your situation. You're passionate, you're enthusiastic and you're waiting to see some changes. And yet, despite your occasional discussions with your friends, colleagues and people in the community, nothing seems to happen. It's so obvious that your local city council, the state legislature or the federal government should modify its practices and yet things remain the same. That's frustrating, right?

Frankly, just talking to your friends, colleagues and people in the community won't get the message across to the policymakers making the decisions. It may be obvious to you that something needs to happen, but it's not obvious to them until you tell them. That's where advocacy comes into play. Through our advocacy efforts, we let our elected officials know what policy proposals are helpful or harmful to our business or cause.

✖ OK, Why Advocate When They Won't Listen Anyway?

"Yeah," you're thinking, "but since they never listen to me that's not very helpful is it?"

Maybe there's a reason for this thinking. You have probably heard someone say, "Politicians won't listen to an average citizen." Or perhaps something along the lines of, "Politicians just like to sit around and argue with each other – they're completely ineffective." Maybe you've even said these things yourself. After all, it's accepted conventional wisdom that politicians are corrupt and government is broken.

Think carefully about these perspectives, though, because there are two sides to every story. If part of the problem is that politicians aren't listening, could a second part of the problem be that people aren't speaking effectively? And while it is true that politicians do argue a great deal, isn't it true that this happens because our system of government was specifically designed to be slow moving, deliberate and argumentative – in a sense, it is reflective of the varying views and interests of the people?

Frankly, if citizens (yes, that's you) aren't willing to make a small effort to communicate with elected officials, they give up all right to whine about "those people in government." So if you want to whine, it's time to step it up and participate. It's time to be an active member of our democracy.

✖ Active Participation in Government: The Basics

How can you be an active participant in government? Achieving this goal requires a commitment to the following three activities: voting, learning about your government and communicating to share your views.

▪ Voting

The right, privilege and responsibility of voting to elect public officials who, in turn, vote to adopt or reject legislation dates back to ancient Greece. Building on fundamental principles developed centuries ago, the United States was designed on the premise that self-government is a natural right of every person and that governments derive their powers from the consent of the governed.

Unfortunately, while we've seen some resurgence in recent Presidential election years, participation by Americans in national elections is very low compared with other democracies. Despite high turnout in the Presidential election of 2008, on average only 25 to 50 percent of eligible citizens in the United States participate in national elections, with an even lower turnout in state and local elections. The presidential elections in 2008, which many characterized as "record" turnout, saw about 61% of eligible Americans making their way to the polls. In other countries these numbers are as high as 96%.

Numerous books and articles examine the reasons for low voter turnout. Our job here is to ensure that effective advocates have the tools they need to be part of the solution, not the problem. Voting requires just three simple steps:

- **Register:** If you want to vote, you must register. In many states, your voter registration forms can be filled out as part of your application for a driver's license. You can visit your local Post Office, government office, or go online to a site like the League of Women Voters (www.lwv.org) and its Voter Information Project (www.vote411.org) to find all the forms you need for registering in your area. If you want to be particularly "edgy" you can go to MTV's Rock the Vote (www.rockthevote.com) for the same information. You only need to register once to be eligible to vote in all primary, general and special elections in your area.

- **Review the Candidates and Make Decisions:** Once you are registered, you will receive a voter guide before the election. Review that guide carefully before election day and make decisions about which candidates you think best reflect your views. You may also want to discuss these issues with friends, review the local papers or review the candidates' websites and campaign materials to help you make an informed decision.

- **Get to the Polls:** On election day, set aside time to get to the polls. Employers are required both by law and, hopefully, a sense of moral responsibility, to allow you time off to go vote. If you will be out of town that day, consider voting absentee or voting early through the mechanisms offered by most local jurisdictions. Check with your local board of elections to see what's possible.

Learning about Your Government

A high school civics class can be a sufficient basis for understanding how government works, but only if it sparks a life-long appetite for staying informed. If you start looking for information about our government -- how it was formed, its history, and current issues -- you will find a great many sources. Listed here are a variety of recommended resources for learning more about how our U.S. Congress was established, how it operates today, and, most important, how its actions can affect your life. Additionally, Chapter 3 of this book details each of the levels and branches of government.

Interested in books on Congress? Look for:

The Federalist Papers
Newspaper articles written by James Madison, Alexander Hamilton, and John Jay during the debates over ratification of the Constitution.

The Almanac of American Politics
Current information on Members of Congress, congressional districts, and the current structure of Congress.

Congressional Quarterly's Congress A to Z
Provides detailed information on Congress in a dictionary format.

Congressional Procedures and the Policy Process
Analysis of how Congress works, legislative procedures, rules, tradition, and policymaking.

Interested in websites related to Congress? Look for:

www.house.gov
The official website of the U.S. House of Representatives.

www.senate.gov
The official website of the U.S. Senate.

www.congress.gov
The Library of Congress website. Through this link you can look up individual bills and information on congressional proceedings. In addition, you will find a link through this site to a tutorial on "how our laws are made." But please, don't read it while operating heavy machinery.

www.votesmart.com
General information on voting records for current and past members of Congress on various issues plus links to political party and media sites.

www.cq.com
The website for Congressional Quarterly, a publication that covers Congress. The site's section on "The American Voter" includes background information on Congress.

www.cspan.com
The website of CSPAN, the cable network that covers Congress. Contains information on the schedule and structure of Congress.

■ **Interested in websites related to your state legislature?**
Use your favorite search engine, such as Google or Yahoo, to search on "[your state] state legislature," where [your state] is replaced with the name of your state. So, for example, if you live in North Dakota, you would search on North Dakota State Legislature. This same search works for your local city council. Simply look for "[your city] city council," or "[your city] city government."

■ **Interested in reviewing or subscribing to a newspaper or other publication that covers Congress? Look for:**

The Washington Post (www.washingtonpost.com): Washington D.C.'s hometown newspaper, with extensive political coverage.

Roll Call (www.rollcall.com): Mainstay of U.S. Congressional coverage.

The Hill (www.thehill.com): Also covers Congress as well as U.S. Politics and Campaigns

Columbia Books (www.columbiabooks.com): Directories and in-depth publications on the Washington lobbying scene

Congressional Quarterly (www.cq.com): In-depth reviews of policy making and up-to-the minute information on Congressional schedules

National Journal (www.nationaljournal.com): Thoughtful analysis of legislative / policy proposals in a variety of issue areas.

Call, Write, or Visit to Share Your Views

Finally, the most important activity an effective advocate can undertake is to actively communicate with elected officials through meetings, phone calls, letters, e-mails -- heck, even send a carrier pigeon if you think that will help! In the following chapters you will learn everything you need to know about getting your message across.

As you begin your advocacy journey, remember that you're in this for the long haul. One phone call or letter does not make an effective advocate. In some cases, it can take years for a policy change to move through the process. Armed with your persistence, determination and, most important, your passion for your cause, you will weather the tempest and doldrums that mark any advocacy campaign and emerge triumphant in

Imagine getting up at 6:30 every morning, Monday through Sunday, and kicking off 14 to 15 hours of non-stop meetings. The meetings are on every issue under the sun -- from trade with foreign countries to traffic conditions to whether the local Post Office should be renamed after Elvis Presley. That pretty accurately describes the life of an elected official with the occasional vacation or day off thrown in.

During a typical week, for example, members of Congress have an extensive schedule of visits, dinners and meetings in their congressional districts or states. They fly to Washington, D.C., where they have more meetings, votes, evening events and, most important, interactions with constituents from their districts and states. Members of the state legislature have similar schedules. And city council members? Forget it. They can't even go to the grocery store without being accosted by constituents.

In the midst of all this competition for attention, getting your message across becomes even more difficult. That's why it's essential that you understand the factors that influence elected officials. Armed with this information, you will be able to craft messages that rise above the chaos.

★ What Influences? The Conventional View

When people think about what influences elected officials, nine out of 10 times their first thought is "money." "Bribes," "gifts," and, occasionally, "sex" usually follow in quick succession. Clearly, skepticism reigns supreme when it comes to our views of how to influence a policymaker.

Let's take a moment to look at some of this conventional wisdom in a new way. Consider the following scenario: a congressman from North Carolina accepts a campaign contribution from the tobacco industry and then- gasp!- votes with tobacco interests. Or, a member of your state legislature actively seeks out an assignment on the committee that regulates the telecommunications industry. Coincidentally, a major telephone company headquartered in her district held a

campaign fundraiser for her at its offices only a few months earlier.

Clearly these officials have been bought off, right? In exchange for campaign contributions, they have agreed to find ways to bestow political favors on their "friends."

But think about it for a minute. Who does the Congressman from North Carolina represent? That's right, it's about a bajillion tobacco farmers. Tobacco is a $7 billion industry in North Carolina. If you represent any part of the state, your efforts to benefit the tobacco industry will translate into real benefits for the people you represent.

Or what about the state legislator with the telecommunications business in her district? One of her obligations as an elected official is to do all she can to ensure the economic health and well-being of those she represents -- including the telecommunications company and the hundreds (or perhaps thousands) of people employed there.

Are these legislators representing the people who contribute to their campaigns? Or the people who live in the district? It's not always as crystal clear as we might think. In fact, financial contributions actually have much less impact on the day-to-day decisions of elected officials than most of us think.

If that's so, then, what about access? Many people argue that financial contributions offer the givers more access to elected officials. Contributors get to hob-nob with candidates and incumbents at fancy events -- events where the rest of us wouldn't even get our foot in the door. And, yes, while it's true that contributors do see elected officials at fundraisers, every day citizens have at least an equal, or in some cases even more powerful, avenue of access. It's called "constituency," and it is, without a doubt, the most powerful factor in influencing elected officials at all levels. We'll talk more about this powerful tool in just a moment.

In the meantime, be assured that we're not expecting your complete acceptance of these arguments. With all the questionable things that happen in politics, people should be somewhat skeptical. All we ask is that you consider the possibility that there may be additional factors that influence elected officials beyond the "money," "bribes,""gifts" and "sex" that we all read so much about in the newspapers.

All that said, don't be discouraged by these arguments from contributing to a candidate's campaign or an organization's Political Action Committee (PAC). Seen in its most positive light, money in the political process helps elect people that already understand and perhaps even agree with your views. In fact, for many organizations, a PAC is an essential component to long-term advocacy success. So go ahead and contribute to those candidates with whom you agree – just don't expect that campaign checks translate into votes and lavish attention.

★ What Doesn't Influence Elected Officials

Before we delve further into the factors that get elected officials to sit up and take notice, let's take a moment to consider what else, beyond the conventional factors listed above, doesn't. Some of the answers might surprise you.

For example, many advocates believe that carefully researched arguments and logical explanations will carry the day. Strictly speaking, logic should, of course, be part of your message. After all, you will need to make a reasoned and well-thought out case for your cause. However, too many people believe that if they just give elected officials the plain and simple truth all will be well. In other words, they believe that "the right answer" will always prevail. Frankly, that's not always the case.

Let's consider an example. Imagine you were advocating to have some parking restrictions imposed in your neighborhood. As a resident, you're finding it increasingly more difficult to find parking on the street. You've noticed that more and more out-of-towners are parking in your area and leaving their cars there all day. You and your neighbors are more vulnerable to late night muggings because of how far you have to walk from your car to your house. In fact, crime in general, including thefts from cars, is on the rise in your area. Your first thought is to gather up the detailed information on number of cars in the neighborhood, number of residents, etc. and present them to your local elected officials. After all, the facts speak for themselves, right? And yet, once you've presented all your facts the local city council rejects your request for more parking restrictions. What happened?

There are at least two reasons why logic often fails. First, the "facts" rarely take up residence on just one side of the issue. In reality there are often multiple sets of facts reflecting multiple priorities. In this situation, for example, businesses in your area may have a competing set of facts -- just as true and just as compelling -- showing that businesses suffer in neighborhoods where there are parking restrictions. Your arguments about the convenience and safety of residents have been pitted against the economic development concerns of the business community.

Second, and perhaps most important, facts aren't people. Elected officials of all kinds respond to the personal stories of the people that are most relevant to them -- their constituents. Dry recitations of numbers and "what's right" are rarely as compelling as a good, old-fashioned anecdote. Not convinced? Which message do you find more persuasive?

Message 1
In the last month, 62% of local residents have had to walk more than three blocks to get from their home to their on-street parking spot at least once. At the same time, late night assaults on residents forced to walk long distances from their car have increased exponentially. We need parking restrictions so that residents can park closer to their homes.

Message 2
Sally Jones, a long time local resident and mother of three, was mugged last night while walking three long blocks from her car to her home. After knocking her to the ground and threatening her with a gun, the assailants fled the scene with her wallet. Sally suffered a broken wrist and concussion in the attack. If she did not have to walk such a long way, she would have been safe. Sally is one of 15 residents who have been accosted in this way in recent months. This is just one reason why we need parking restrictions.

Hopefully, if I've made my point correctly, you found the second argument most persuasive. And yet the first argument makes the same points and potentially applies to more people. But it's missing the personal component that captures our attention.

Another technique that doesn't work as well as one might think is using poll information to make a point. That doesn't seem right, though, does it? How many times have you heard "all politicians ever do is follow the polls"? In truth, though, it doesn't really matter to an elected official if 65% of Americans say "X" or 72% of Americans oppose "Y." What they really care about is what 65% of their own constituents think. Those are the polls that matter.

Believe it or not, people in different parts of the country or even in different parts of a city don't always share the same views. In our parking restriction scenario, for example, advocates might be tempted to argue that poll results from around the country demonstrate that, in general, people support parking restrictions in their neighborhoods. But a local city council member won't care what people around the country think. He or she will care only about the views of the people he or she represents.

★ Other Factors of Influence

OK, so if money, logic and polls don't work as well as we always thought they did, what does? Take a moment to think about and write down a few things that you think influence elected officials. Chances are, you wrote down some version of the following:

Personal Relationships

Believe it or not, elected officials are people too! They have friends, family members -- even pets. They often seek advice and information from these sources (maybe not so much from the pets). In fact, just try to get through a day in a policymaker's office without talking to a spouse or child. Staff members are also included in this category. In many legislative venues they serve as the policymaker's right hand and most trusted advisors. Ignore them at your peril. You'll learn more about the staff in later chapters.

The Message

What you say to elected officials is actually important. Consider the differences between the following two messages:

Message 1

"Hey there, Congressman X. I don't actually live or work in the area you represent, but since all you people here in the state legislature work for us taxpayers, I figured you have to listen to me and do what I say, right? I mean, I'm the boss, aren't I? So, I'd really like you to do something about the price of gasoline. It's too high. It needs to be fixed. Don't expect me to vote for you or give you any money until I see gasoline at less than $3 per gallon."

Message 2

"Congressman X, my name is Jane Doe and I live in your district. Recent increases in the price of gasoline have directly and negatively impacted my ability to manage my pizza delivery business. In fact, the average cost of delivering a pizza has risen from $1.25 per customer to $2.00 per customer in just six months, all as a result of the sharp increase in fuel. My overall costs have increased by 30% and I am concerned that I will have to lay off some of my employees. I ask you to help small business owners like me by voting to reduce the state level taxes on gasoline and providing more incentives for fuel efficient cars. Thank you for your time."

Regardless of your own views of gasoline prices, which message did you personally find more persuasive? Remember that elected officials are people too and will likely share your perspectives on what messages resonate. To be most effective, your messages must be relevant, personal, thoughtful and specific. Later chapters of this book will offer insights into developing a winning message.

The Media

Media coverage of events will often have an influence on what elected officials talk about in hearings and introduce as legislation. But the good news here is that "the media" doesn't always mean the New York Times, USA Today or the major television networks. In fact, elected officials often pay closest attention to the weekly or even monthly community newspapers that may have a smaller circulation but are closest to the people they represent. An important part of any effective advocacy effort will be to ensure that your message makes its way into these publications. Later chapters in this book will show you how.

Personal Interests and Passions

Every elected official has a policy issue they love: something they campaigned on or something on which they've introduced legislation. Effective advocates will figure out what those interests are and then frame their message in those terms. In other words, rather than talking exclusively about your issue or cause, sometimes it's better to talk about something you know your audience is interested in, and then connect your message to that.

How does this work? Imagine you want to ask your state representative to support more funding for research on childhood cancers. You could tell your personal story and explain the importance of this issue to you. Or, you could do a little research and learn that the elected official has introduced a bill to increase reimbursement rates for cancer drugs. Now you can start your pitch with a reference to the representative's work on cancer drugs and the need for more research on the differences in treatment options for children with cancer versus adults. Your overall message becomes significantly more powerful when you connect it to the work your representative is already doing in this area.

Learning something about your audience and framing your message in terms they understand and care about will greatly enhance your chances of success. We'll provide details on what you need to know and where to find out in subsequent chapters.

The Most Important Factor

What's the one thing you must have in order to influence an elected official? The one, end-all, be-all, essential element to your effective advocacy efforts? The one thing that no advocacy campaign can do without? It's a constituency connection.

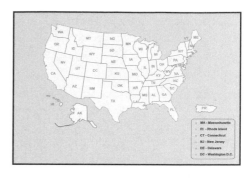

Every elected official represents a very specific geographic area within which lives an important group of people: his or her constituents. Whether a city council member, a state legislator or a Member of the U.S. Congress, the highest and most important obligation is to the people he or she represents. That's why the most common phrase heard in any elected officials' office is "how does this impact my constituents." It is the framework through which all decisions are made. We'll focus on constituency in subsequent chapters, specifically how to find out who represents you as well as how to build a campaign based on constituency connections.

In short, policymakers and their staffs receive hundreds of pieces of mail, hundreds of phone calls, and dozens of visitors every day, the vast majority of which seek to influence policy. But the communications that matter the most are those from constituents. Both members and staff will do everything in their power to carve time out of their busy schedules to meet with constituents, talk with them on the phone, or draft letters in response to their questions. Through the constituency connection, you demonstrate your relevance to your elected officials -- and set the stage for a truly powerful advocacy experience.

"I'm just a bill, just a lonely old bill..."
Chances are, if you were alive during the 1970's and 1980's, you heard some version of "School House Rock." You know -- the one where the singing bill talks about the legislative process. I always found it very heartwarming when the bill actually became a law ("I'm a law now!").

At the time, I did not realize how rarely that happens. In fact, of the 10,000+ bills that are introduced in a two-year congressional session, only about 4 to 5 percent actually become law. At the state level, the percentage of bills that pass is usually a little higher, sometimes as high as 25 percent.

Your first thought may be "well, that certainly is a dismal percentage" -- and it is. You might even think that our system of government is clearly broken. If our legislatures pass such a small percentage of what they introduce, then clearly something, somewhere, isn't working, right?

However, the percentage of bills passed is not really a good measure of the success of a legislative body because -- and I know this will shock you -- legislatures aren't actually designed to pass legislation. They are designed to deliberate, argue and actually fight about policy initiatives -- and they do an awfully good job of that.

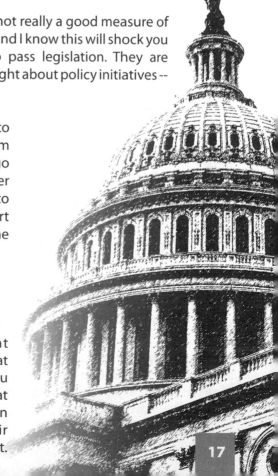

The idea that legislatures aren't designed to pass legislation is just one of the "paradigm shifts" that any advocate will need to undergo to be truly effective. In this chapter we'll cover more of those interesting things you need to know about government before you start trying to make a difference (but only the interesting things, I promise).

★ The Three Levels of Government

Effective advocates understand that government activity takes place on one of at least three levels (sometimes more). If you think about it, the only way you'll get what you want is to ask the right people. Too often advocates waste time delivering their messages to the wrong level of government.

Members of Congress or the state legislature aren't going to be able to help with getting a stop sign installed on your street. Likewise, your mayor can't really do anything about the Alternative Minimum Tax (in fact, he or she is probably just as irritated about it as you are).

Starting with an understanding of which level of government can help you achieve your goal allows you to evaluate the political environment and develop a message that truly resonates. We'll discuss the details of developing a winning message in later chapters. For now, suffice to say that knowing the "state of play" in the level of government you're reaching out to will greatly increase your chances of success.

What are these three levels? First, there's the "local" level: think of your city council, mayor, county commission, local agencies such as transportation or housing or a regional organization. Government activity at this level is usually confined to very narrow geographic areas. For example, issues relating to your garbage collection service, zoning or building permits or property tax rates are usually very local types of functions.

The next level is the "state" level: think of, well, your state government. This would include your governor, your state House and Senate (except Nebraska – you just have one) and state agencies. Policies discussed at this level will generally impact the entire state or large portions of the state. A few state level examples of government activity include funding for and management of state parks, building and maintenance of state highways and, of course, those lovely state income taxes that many people pay.

Finally, there's the federal level. This is where advocates get to play with Congress, the President and federal agencies like the EPA and the IRS. Government activity at this level is generally very broad in scope. In fact, the Constitution states (and I'm paraphrasing here) that the federal government can do anything "not reserved for the states." This work includes federal income taxes, creation and funding of national programs like Social Security and Medicare / Medicaid, as well as trade and interactions with foreign countries.

Throughout the book, we'll talk more about the three levels of government. The main point here is that in order to be effective you must know which level of government can help you achieve your goal. Sometimes, that's easy. If you want to have your sidewalk repaired, that's almost always your local government. If you want to see changes at a state park, the state government is the place to go. And, if you want to see changes in the Alternative Minimum Tax, I'm afraid you'll have to deal with the federal government.

⭐ When It's Not So Easy

Unfortunately, complicated funding and policy programs don't always make that easy because so much of the work done by one level of government depends on, or is impacted by, the activity at another level. For example:

- Imagine you'd like to see your local school provide more funding for the school library. You've noticed that there's no full-time staff person, no computers and the resources in the library are outdated. Since it's a local school, you should probably start with your local principal, administrator or board of education. But then you find that as a result of state funding measures, the amount of money going to the school specifically for libraries has been dramatically reduced. At the same time, you learn that recently passed federal laws require the schools to invest more funds in special education, testing supplies and teacher training. All three policies at all three levels may need to be changed to help you achieve your goal.

- Or, perhaps you'd like to see stringent EPA air quality regulations that impact your ability to run your business reduced or eliminated. Since the regulations are from the EPA, that seems to be the most logical place to start. But, in many cases, states and even localities have passed conforming legislation to comply with the requirements of federal laws. You might find yourself out of the EPA frying pan and into the state environmental regulatory agency fire.

What's an advocate to do? Whatever you do, don't give up. While you may need to rein in your expectations, there is almost always some way that your direct passion and enthusiasm for a particular cause can make a positive difference. For example, you may find yourself partnering with other concerned citizens to advocate at all three levels of government. Or, you may find that by focusing on one level, you can make an incremental improvement in the situation you're trying to address.

In short, the most important things to keep asking yourself about the three levels of government are some variation of:

- Can the people I'm talking to in government office X, Y or Z help me with at least one part of my problem?
  OR
- If I want to solve problem X, what level of government should I approach?

⭐ The Three Branches of Government

Another important "three" to keep in mind is the three branches of government (these things always come in threes: why? I don't know). I'll bet, though, that the last time you heard about the three branches of government was sometime in high school. You probably thought to yourself: "I'm never going to use this, so why am I learning it?" Good news! This previously not-so-useful information will come in handy in your advocacy efforts. Understanding just a little about the three branches of government will help you better relate to your audience – and ultimately lead to greater success.

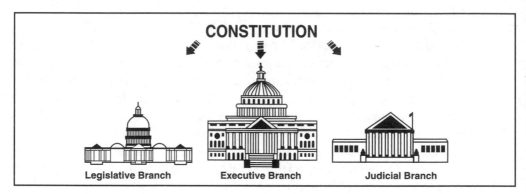

You may recall from your dreary social studies class that the three branches of government are the judicial branch, the executive branch and the legislative branch. The relative strengths and weaknesses of each have ebbed and flowed over the years, and scholars disagree as to which branch is the "most important." We will not be resolving that dilemma. Rather, our goal is twofold. First, we want look at each of these branches through the "advocacy lens" to determine where and how citizen advocates can have the most say.

Second, and perhaps most important, we need to understand why we are so focused on what happens in Congress, state legislatures and city councils. The short answer is that while citizen participation can and does occur at all levels and within all branches of government, citizens will find their strongest power lies in their interactions with the legislative branch.

That said, we ignore the other branches at our peril – so let's take a quick look at the judicial and executive branches before delving into the legislative branch.

⭐ The Judicial Branch

The judicial branch refers to the court systems of our country, either the U.S. Federal Courts or the court systems of the various states. Individual communities have local court systems as well, of course. These tend to be agents of or managed by the state judicial system.

The job of the judicial branch at any level is broadly to interpret laws, but each system has very different jurisdictions. For example, because most laws that impact citizens on a day-to-day basis (criminal code violations, traffic laws, etc.) are state laws, the state courts have very broad jurisdictions. Most "garden variety" burglaries, traffic violations and interpersonal disputes play out at this level.

The federal courts, on the other hand, may consider only those cases that raise questions of federal law. These might include international cases where the U.S. is involved, issues related specifically to federal laws, such as maritime or bankruptcy law, or cases that involve large-scale disputes between residents of different states. Some of these issues might rise to the level of the federal Supreme Court, which interprets questions relating to the Constitution.

Those who constructed our nation's government over 200 years ago intended the federal court system, and specifically the Supreme Court, to act as a "check" on the powers of the other two branches of government. The Justices of the Supreme Court can even find federal or state legislation or acts of the President to be unconstitutional – and nothing short of a constitutional amendment will change their mind.

What can advocates do with this branch?
At first glance, it may seem as though an individual advocate might not have a tremendous role to play with either the state or federal court system -- except to avoid it if at all possible. After all, everyone knows that you need to be a lawyer, or know a great deal about the law, to make effective arguments in a court case.

Wise advocates, however, will step back and think carefully about other potential points of access into this branch. While the average citizen may not be able to prepare a legal case that would sway a judge, this does not mean that we cannot have an impact. In fact, citizen advocates can dramatically alter the judicial environment and, as a result, the decisions made through this branch of government. How? Here are just a few examples:

- Advocating for or against the

confirmation of a particular judge: As an example, many states and the federal Supreme Court place the power of appointing and confirming the justices of the court in the hands of the legislature and/or Governor. And who are the legislature and Governor responsible to? That's right, their constituents. Utilizing your influence as a voter with those who will eventually vote to confirm or deny a specific justice can have a dramatic impact on the ultimate shape of the court.

Not sure about your ability to influence? Just ask would-be Supreme Court Justice Robert Bork. He was nominated by President Reagan to serve on the Court in 1987. The matter was turned over to the U.S. Senate, which must approve any nominees to the Court. Citizens, particularly those involved with an advocacy campaign spearheaded by the ACLU and People for the American Way, contacted their Senators in droves to express their concerns about the nomination. Bork's nomination was ultimately rejected by a vote of 42 to 58, with many Republican Senators (members of the President's own party) joining to vote down the nominee.

- Participating in an election campaign in support or opposition to a judge: Other states hold elections for judicial positions. As voters, citizens can play a role in determining whether a particular person will or will not be appointed.

- Assisting non-profits representing your interests at the courts: Many non-profit organizations at the state and federal level become involved in court cases as part of their efforts to further their cause. The American Civil Liberties Union (ACLU), for example, is well known for its active judicial activities on behalf of free speech. The Humane Society of the United States often takes to the state and federal courts to enforce and strengthen animal welfare laws. Becoming involved with these organizations in this type of work can have a direct impact on what decisions come out of the courts.

In short, the key to being an effective judicial branch advocate is to focus on your citizen power in those ways and on those audiences where you are most likely to make a difference. In the case of the judicial branch, trying to make direct arguments (unless you've been trained by many, many years of school to do so) simply will not be as effective as exerting your influence in other ways – say, through the legislature or outside interest groups. Throughout the course of this book, you'll learn the best ways of applying that pressure to achieve maximum results.

★ The Executive Branch

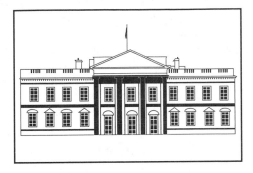

The executive branch of government administrates and implements the laws passed by the legislature. At the state level, the executive branch is comprised of the state governor and the various state agencies. At the federal level, the President of the United States heads the executive branch and is responsible for the actions and activities of the various federal agencies. When the state legislature or the U.S. Congress passes a law, it is the job of the various agencies and divisions within the related executive branch to set up the programs and processes necessary to ensure proper implementation of the law.

How do you know whether you're dealing with an executive branch entity? Well, the terms "Department of…" or "Agency" usually offer your first clue. So if you're dealing with the "[your state] Department of Transportation", that's usually the executive branch agency in your state responsible for implementing and administering transportation laws.

I'll admit that from this rather simple description it sounds like the staff in executive branch agencies are little more than lackeys who simply do the bidding of the legislature. This perspective, however, does not tell the whole story. In fact, executive branch agencies have a great deal of power to determine the structure and day-to-day operations of the programs or policies approved by the legislature. Let's look at a couple examples:

Let's say your state legislature passes a bill that designates a certain area of the state as a state park. The legislative language may include details on the specific geographic area, the potential uses of the park and even a name. However, it is the state agency managing the parks that will likely determine important factors such as when the park will be available to the public, where and how facilities will be built, what the hours will be, and what fees to charge for accessing park services. Your experience as a citizen using the park will probably be far more dramatically impacted by the decisions of the agency than the legislature itself (of course, you might not be able to even use the park without the legislature's involvement).

Or, consider what happens when the U.S. Congress establishes policies to reduce the levels of certain air-borne contaminants. While Congress will likely have a great deal to say about what kinds of contaminants should be regulated and what the target levels should be reduced to over time, the EPA will determine the full impact of the program, answering questions such as what technologies might be used to achieve the goals and what measurement techniques should be used to determine that targets have been reached. These types of decisions will likely have far more impact on the day-to-day operations of a coal-fired plant, for example, than the broad guidelines established in the U.S. Congress. Again, though, the coal-fired plant might not have been impacted at all if Congress had not passed the legislation.

Clearly, in its role as administrator and implementer of the laws, an executive branch agency can enormously impact how individual citizens or businesses will be affected by legislative policies. In addition, unique executive branch powers such as the presidential or governor's "veto" can serve to dramatically limit the power of the legislature. So how can we have a say in the workings of this somewhat mysterious branch of government?

What can advocates do with this branch?

Picture, if you will, a typical government bureaucrat. Many of us would imagine a Caucasian, perhaps middle-aged man with a certain attitude that exudes "lack of helpfulness." While these individuals certainly do exist within executive branch agencies, for the most part those who choose this life of public service really do want to help people. Unfortunately, many of them are caught in internally created "intransigent bureaucracies."

What? Our government is supposed to have bureaucracies? Chances are you thought they were an unfortunate side-effect. In fact, a bureaucracy is simply "A formal, hierarchical organization with many levels in which tasks, responsibilities, and authority are delegated among individuals, offices, or departments, held together by a central administration." They are the structures that executive branch agencies use to ensure that the policies passed by the legislature are properly implemented. The problems with bureaucracies is that sometimes the people in and around them become more committed to the rules and regulations governing programs than they do the actual benefits of and original reasons for the programs themselves. So how can an advocate make a difference in this environment? Here are some ideas:

- Participate in the Executive Agency's Public Comment Process: Almost all executive agencies, from your local Department of Water and Sewer to the U.S. Internal Revenue Service, are required to offer an opportunity for public comment whenever they propose a change to their rules. Anyone with an opinion is allowed to file a comment and anyone with an informed opinion based on some level of expertise may actually be heard. Agencies actually review these comments pretty carefully and may use the more provocative and trustworthy information to make changes to what was originally proposed.

- Work on the Executive Agency Through Your Elected Representatives: There's one group of people that those government bureaucrats will pay some attention, and that's the group that approves the agency's budget. Your local, state or federal representatives have an amazing ability to gain the attention of agency officials. Utilize your own amazing power to be heard by your elected officials to enlist their assistance in "cutting through" the red tape.

A constituent of one of the Members of Congress I worked for understood this approach very well. He strongly believed that the U.S. Department of Commerce, which makes decisions about where to post weather radar systems, should post such a system at a specific location in our district. He argued that a radar system at that location could provide information about weather patterns to a range of business interests, all of whom could really use the information. Local transport companies, for example, would want to know about potential disruptions in air traffic, while local farmers could use the radar system to plan their activities days or even weeks ahead. Our constituent had made his case to the Department of Commerce directly with very little luck, so he turned to our office. Granted, as a 24-year-old staff person I knew next to nothing about weather radar – but I sure knew who the business interests in our district were. I talked to both the constituent and the local branch of the Department of Commerce to learn more about the benefits of the system and shared this information with my boss. He took steps to ensure that a system was eventually installed.

The lesson here? Instead of beating your head against the wall of the "intransigent bureaucracy," look for the most effective ways to apply your true power. You may be surprised at the results.

★ The Legislative Branch

It's no accident that each of the discussions above about "how advocates can be effective" mentions the legislative branch. This is because the legislative branch is widely recognized as the most representative and, believe it or not, the most responsive to the concerns of citizens.

What do legislatures do?

Legislatures at all levels create the laws that govern the jurisdiction that particular legislature serves. Local city councils develop laws that impact the city (such as zoning codes or housing policies), state legislatures work on laws that impact the entire state while the U.S. Congress is responsible for laws affecting the entire nation. In addition, legislatures often manage the "purse strings" of their jurisdiction. In other words, the other two branches of government rely on the legislature to provide their funding. As you might imagine, this often gives the legislature a great deal of influence over what goes on in the executive and judicial branches.

Local city councils, county commissions, state legislatures and the U.S. Congress are examples of legislative branch institutions. Most of the state legislatures are structured similarly to the U.S. Congress, with two "houses" (often called a House and a Senate). In some cases either the organization traditionally thought of as the "House" or the entire legislature itself may be called a "General Assembly." Despite these differences in nomenclature, for our purposes, it's useful to think of most of the state legislatures as "bicameral" (i.e., two houses) institutions. One exception is the state of Nebraska which, for reasons of its own, decided to have a unicameral (i.e., one house) legislature. At the local level (such as the city or county), the law-making body is usually just one group.

The people who are elected are generally referred to as "council members," "commissioners," "legislators," "members of the Assembly," "Congresspeople," "Representative" or "Senator" depending on the level of government in which they serve, and their respective house, where applicable. When you hear these terms bandied about, you can feel fairly certain that you're dealing with a legislature.

The most important thing for an effective advocate to remember is that while they may all have different structures, every legislative organization has one thing in common: each is comprised of people elected by citizens to represent their interests. As such, each is ultimately responsible to and reliant on the perspectives of those they represent.

Granted, sometimes it seems like the elected representatives in our legislature do not take the responsibility to represent the views of their constituents very seriously. That's where elections come in handy: if you're not feeling as though the people in the legislature take their responsibilities seriously, don't just sit back and complain – vote the bums out! In fact, your power to vote gives you an amazing hold over your legislators. The framers of the Constitution saw the ability of citizens to choose their own government as the ultimate "check and balance" on all three branches of government.

Too bad so many of us squander that power – but not you, right?

What can advocates do with this branch?
Besides "voting the bums out," advocates can do a great deal to influence this most receptive of audiences. In subsequent chapters, we'll outline very specific ways to successfully approach legislatures, including what to know before you go, how to develop messages that resonate, and the importance of follow-up. For now, let's look at the four overall principles for getting heard with this branch of government.

Four Overall Principles for Effective Legislative Advocacy

1. Know What You Want
First, you've got to know what you want. As we'll discuss in the next chapter, your communications with elected officials will be effective only if you have a specific goal in mind. Too often, advocates spend a great deal of time telling their happy or tragic stories without any idea of how a legislator can help them. To be successful you'll need to know a little about what an elected official can (and cannot) do for you.

2. Know Who You're Talking To
Second, you've got to know something about your audience. Your voice has the most power with those elected officials who represent the area where you live, work or serve others. You will be known to these officials as a "constituent" and this "power of constituency" is an amazing power (it's not quite a super-power yet, but we're working on it).

The good news is that as a resident of the United States of America, you are a constituent of many different elected leaders including your local city council member, your mayor, your state legislators (usually a member of the state House and Senate) and three members of the U.S. Congress (your one House Representative and two Senators). You are also a constituent of the President of the United States! Who knew you had such sway over the workings of government?

3. Know How to Talk to Them
Third, you'll need to develop messages that resonate and you'll need to deliver those messages in a meaningful way. In subsequent chapters, we'll take a look at the elements of a winning message, the benefits and downsides of various delivery methods (such as in-person meetings and e-mails) and the tricks to getting your communications noticed among the thousands coming in to an elected official's office every day.

4. Know How to Follow-Up

Finally, you'll need to apply all the persistence, tenacity and down-right stubbornness you can to the problem of getting legislators to listen. In a perfect world, you would simply be able to reach out to your elected officials with a relevant, compelling story, make your ask and then watch the wheels of government turn. In the real world it's not quite that easy. But, the more persistence you demonstrate, the more likely your elected officials are to take you seriously. Once you show them you know how to "play the game," you'll find that gaining their attention and support will be much, much easier.

Are you ready to learn those rules? Let's go!

4 | KNOWING WHAT YOU WANT

The first rule in any advocacy effort is to be sure you know what you want. Only when you know your specific goal can you be sure that you're talking to the right audience. For example, if you know that you want a new park in your neighborhood, you're probably going to need to approach your city or county government. On the other hand, if you know you want to change the way federal tax laws apply to your business (and businesses like yours), you'll need to reach out to the federal government.

Your association or employer, where applicable, is *always* a good first stop for identifying "what you want." These entities have done all the "heavy lifting" to position your issues for success in the legislature. They've sifted through the thousands of bills that are introduced and have often worked closely with legislators to ensure that some of those bills are changes in law that will benefit your particular policy perspective. These organizations may include a Government Relations or Advocacy section on their websites, or will provide up-to-the-minute information on the policy issues that will most impact your situation. You may even receive "action alerts" or other updates outlining the specific "asks" upon which you should be focused. These materials are invaluable in helping to answer the "what can my legislators do for me" question.

★ What do I do if there is No Ask? What if My Elected Officials Just Need "Educating?"

Your first instinct (as has been the first instinct of many an advocate before you) may be that you should spend some time "educating" your elected officials on your issue. People like to think that if they simply help the elected official understand the benefits of a new neighborhood park (or change in the tax code), the elected official will become enthusiastically excited about the prospect and get on board. These conversations usually go something like this:

> **Advocate:** "Hi! My name is Sally Jones and I'm here to educate you on the benefits of neighborhood parks. Neighborhood parks are good for children, wildlife and families. We like neighborhood parks. They help us connect with nature."
>
> **Council member:** "Great! I like parks too. I remember when I was just a little girl I used to love nothing better than to go to the park."
>
> **Advocate:** "I'm so glad you share our views on parks. We look forward to talking with you more on this topic."
>
> **Council member:** "Good. I need to run to my next meeting now, but I hope you'll stay in touch."

The advocate leaves thinking, "Great, the council member is really on our side!" The council member leaves thinking, "I wonder what that was all about?" Months pass and the council member doesn't do anything about the new park or, worse, she votes against the park budget. The advocates are bewildered. "But we thought you liked parks, council member!" they grumble. And the council member, equally bewildered, says in response, "Sure, I like parks, but no one ever asked me about public funding for parks. I've always been very fiscally conservative."

This whole confused episode could have been avoided if only the advocates had asked for something specific. They learned the hard way that trying to "educate" your elected officials without asking for something specific is like trying to educate a middle-schooler without telling them it will be on the test. It goes in one ear and out the other. Yet, too many people think that elected officials need or want to learn all the ins and outs of a particular issue.

Don't get me wrong. I'm not suggesting that elected officials can't or won't learn new things (well, some won't, but that's a different story). In fact, many elected officials ask to be occasionally "briefed" on important issues they might have to vote on in the future. What I am suggesting is that too often, advocates will focus on "educating" elected officials to the exclusion of doing anything else.

If you think about it, what is the purpose of "education?" There are usually a number of goals, such as getting students to learn to think critically or providing them with the skills and information they need to undertake a specific task or career. Through education, some people become experts on issues and help others learn about them.

However, elected officials do not need, nor could they possibly utilize, a thorough "education" on all the issues they deal with on a daily basis. Try for just one moment to imagine every issue on the planet, whether it's transportation, animal welfare, energy, communications, health care or trade with China. These are the issues that elected officials deal with all the time. There is no possible way they can be as "educated" or knowledgeable on those issues as the transportation engineers, veterinarians, utility managers, telephone manufacturers, doctors or the Chinese. While they should be familiar with some of the intricacies of an issue, the most important thing they need to know is who the relevant "educated expert" on that issue is, and how that issue relates to the elected official's constituents.

In addition, let's be honest: when we use the term "educate" in the political environment, don't we really mean "propagandize" (as in, "We need to propagandize the U.S. Congress on this issue.")? As crass as it sounds, our ultimate goal is not the benign "education" of our elected officials. We want them to agree with us, right? So how do we achieve that goal?

✪ Make the Ask

The first step is to make sure that they're listening to us. Asking for something specific achieves that goal. It sends the signal to the elected official that he or she should pay attention to what you're talking about because it will be on the test -- and the test is their upcoming re-election campaign. In essence, through a specific ask, you're saying, "Hey, Congressman, I am going to evaluate your performance on this issue. I hope you get a passing grade!"

In addition, making an ask lets the people you're dealing with know that you know how to play the game. You see, any elected official worth his or her salt will try to agree with you as much as possible. When you don't ask for something specific, this becomes very easy for them, as seen in the parks example above. The elected official wants to be supportive and agreeable so she talks about her own positive experiences with parks. No one asks her anything more specific so she looks like the good guy (or gal, in this case).

However, if, in that example, the advocates had politely said something like "given your strong support of local parks we hope you'll be willing to support a funding level of XYZ for a new park in our neighborhood," the elected official would then have had to stop and think about whether that level of funding fit in with her fiscally conservative views. In other words, she wouldn't have gotten away with the "I love parks" statement – and the advocates would have had a better idea of where she stood on the issue.

★ Isn't it Pushy to Always Be "Asking"?

People often take issue with me on this point. They say that they don't want to always be asking for something. Sometimes, they just want to say "thank you" to an elected official. I'm all for saying "thank you" (hey my mother raised my right). In fact, you can read all about the importance of thank yous in Chapter 12. If you are communicating with your elected officials frequently, and by that I mean once a month or more, you should absolutely use one of those opportunities to thank your elected officials, especially if they've been very useful. In general, though, the effective advocate will remember that one of the main reasons why elected officials don't do what we want is because we never ask.

In addition, remember that elected officials and their staff expect you to present them with a particular action you'd like them to take. They know that you're probably there to ask for something and they're ready for it. In fact, if you don't ask for something specific, they may be left thinking "now that was a big waste of my time." And don't ever kid yourself that those on the other side of your issue aren't asking. Everyone's asking – you should be prepared to do so as well.

Now, that said, your ask doesn't always have to be something "aggressive", like "vote for this legislation, or else." I refer to these as "policy asks" and, while you'll want to ask for something like this eventually, you don't always have to begin there. In fact, if you're still uncomfortable about the whole idea of the ask, you can start with something that will benefit the elected official as much as, or more than, it will benefit you. These are what I call relationship-building asks. They might include asking an elected official to visit your facility, office, building or neighborhood or asking them to write an article for your newsletter. You've still moved away from "educating" the elected official and in to the more concrete realm of asking – but it's an easier ask and you're far more likely to get a yes.

Let's look in more detail at each of these types of asks:

✪ Policy Asks

When we think about "advocacy," the asks we usually focus on are "policy asks." These include things like "vote for this bill" or "reduce this particular tax." Before making a policy ask, though, it's always a good idea to know whether the people you're talking to can even do what you want. Recall the ideas from Chapter 3 about the structure of government and the descriptions of which branch does what. That overview will be useful as we look at the kinds of things that elected officials (i.e., members of the legislative branches of government) can and cannot do for you at the federal, state, and local level.

What types of policy actions can legislators take?

Whether dealing with the local, state or federal level, there are a pretty specific set of policy-related or "official" actions that a legislator can take. These include:

▪ **Introducing legislation**
One of the legislator's main roles is to propose changes to laws and/or funding for programs within the jurisdiction they serve. So, for example, if you believe that businesses operating in the city should recycle trash, you might ask your city council member to propose a recycling law. Or, if you believe your state government should invest more of the state's budget in libraries, you might ask your state legislator to propose an increase in funding as part of the budget process. Similarly, if you believe that low-income individuals should receive a credit on their federal taxes, you might ask your U.S. Member of Congress to introduce legislation on that issue. The act of proposing changes to the law is the same at all three levels. However, what's ultimately introduced and eventually passed will impact only that particular jurisdiction. The effective advocate understands the scale of his or her asks and reaches out to the appropriate legislator.

▪ **Cosponsor existing legislation**
In addition to introducing their own legislation, in most legislative organizations legislators can cosponsor or otherwise formally express support for policy changes proposed by other legislators. In looking at the examples above, advocates may ask other members of the council to express support for the recycling bill. They may ask other state legislators to support the library funding request. Or they may ask other Members of the U.S. Congress to cosponsor the low-income tax credit legislation. Having cosponsors on a bill is an important way of demonstrating that the idea is relatively non-controversial and will dramatically increase the bill's chances of eventual passage. If you're going to ask an elected official to cosponsor another's legislation, it is

important to know that in cases of a "bicameral" (i.e., two house) legislature --
such as exists with most state legislatures and the U.S. Congress -- members of
one house cannot cosponsor or formally endorse legislation in the other house.
This means, for example, that a member of the U.S. House cannot cosponsor
Senate legislation and vice-versa.

Vote for or against bills at various stages in the process

The act of voting is the "lifeblood" of the legislative process and of democracies
in general. Legislators can introduce all the legislation they want, but in order
for it to have any real impact, it will eventually need to be voted on. In fact,
legislation that successfully makes it all the way through the process to become
a law must be voted upon several times, usually at least once in a Committee
environment and then by the entire organization. In the city council
environment noted above, for example, the proposed recycling law will
probably have to go through a vote of some sort in a Committee of the city
council before being voted on by the entire city council itself. When dealing
with bicameral legislative organizations like most state legislatures and the U.S.
Congress, both houses must pass legislation by vote through a Committee and
each house. Then the two houses must agree on how they will reconcile any
differences between the two versions of the legislation before it can be sent to
the head of the executive branch for signing or veto. Believe it or not, asking
your elected officials to vote for legislation you support (or against legislation
you oppose) can have an enormous impact on the final outcome.

Interact with other branches of government on your behalf

Helping individuals understand and work through the various executive
branch agencies is an important but often overlooked activity of the legislative
branch. Recall from Chapter 3 that the executive branch agencies are the ones
that implement the laws passed by the legislature. If you've ever had trouble
getting your Social Security check, signing up for Medicare, or dealing with the
IRS or state tax office, you know that that's not always as simple as it sounds.
Fortunately, your elected officials can often help you solve individual and
business problems with agencies.

At the U.S. Congressional level, for example, every Member of Congress
employs staff people called "case workers." This staffers work with individuals in
their district or state (in the case of the Senate) to solve individual problems,
such as problems with Veterans benefits or getting disability checks. Many state
legislators have similar capabilities. If they don't have a dedicated staff person,
they can often at least send a letter to the agency in question on your behalf.
Likewise, local city council members can also play a role in sorting out problems
with local agencies. The key is to approach members of the legislature that

correspond to the agency with whom you're having a problem. Members of the state legislature, for example, aren't going to be able to help you much with a federal agency like the EPA -- and Members of the U.S. Congress won't be able to do much with the state environmental agency.

★ What Legislative Branch Offices (like Congress, the State Legislature or Your City Council) Generally Cannot or Should Not do for You

Clearly, legislators can do a great deal for the people they represent. They can introduce changes to the laws and funding proposals within the jurisdiction they serve, they can show support for other legislative initiatives, they can vote for or against legislation and they can interact with other branches of government. Believe it or not, though, sometimes people ask for things that their legislators can't help them with. Then they get frustrated at the "unresponsiveness" of government. The effective advocate, on the other hand, knows that jurisdictional issues, ethics rules, work-load limitations, and plain old common sense limits the actions your legislative representatives can take on your behalf.

Let's look at some of the things NOT to ask your legislators for:

Special Actions Favoring You or Your Business

Your elected officials cannot guarantee a government or private contract, grant, or other government or private action that favors your business. This is illegal, unethical and, in fact, some former state legislators and Members of Congress are in jail for this very crime. Elected officials generally shy away from any implication that they are using their influence to extract money from an agency or private entity for a constituent. However, your legislators can send a general letter of support for an existing grant request, saying something like, "I hope you will give this grant request every consideration." Such a letter would not say, "Please approve this grant request."

Do people really ask for this kind of thing? You bet they do. Here's one memorable example from my days as a young Congressional staffer. Some constituents were moving their carry-out restaurant to a new location. They were concerned because the new location, unlike the old location, did not have the advantage of having a Post Office next door. Seems that the Post Office generated a lot of foot traffic. So they asked their congressional office to arrange to move the Post Office so that it would be near their new location. For a congressional office to act on this request would be highly unethical as well as impractical. Clearly, this is an extreme example. But congressional offices frequently receive requests for specific favorable government actions.

Legal / Tax / Real Estate Advice

Your elected officials cannot help you with specific legal or tax questions, such as whether you can claim certain deductions, or the detailed legal implications of real estate transactions. These questions should be referred to a lawyer, an accountant, or the IRS. In addition, your elected officials can't give you any guarantees on whether a particularly favorable or unfavorable piece of legislation will or won't be passed in time to coincide with your tax or accounting year. However, it is always appropriate to contact your representatives to seek changes to a law you think is unfair or unwise.

Personal / Scholastic Favors

Your elected officials cannot draft your term paper for you, or send you detailed government reports on a moment's notice. However, with about two to three weeks' notice, your representatives can send you reports from government research agencies about specific research topics. Do not follow the example set by a constituent who called in to our office one day wanting all the background information we might have from a variety of sources on a very controversial forestry issue having to do with building roads, although she wasn't quite sure what it was about, or when a vote on it might have occurred. And she wanted the information that day via fax for her class that evening. Our office simply could not help her because she had not given us enough notice. These types of requests are made about once a week.

Issues Relating to Other Levels of Government

Often, people will write asking their U.S. representative or senator to cosponsor or introduce legislation that is being considered at the state level. However, as we learned in Chapter 3, members of one legislative organization do not cosponsor, debate, vote on, or formally consider legislation at another level. So a Member of Congress will play no role in legislative initiatives at the state level. Likewise, a number of things are regulated solely at the state or local level (local utilities and zoning codes for example). While Members of the House and Senate may play a role in national legislation to set the framework for how electricity is regulated, or how localities manage their land, they play no formal role in the actual regulation.

In short, if you ask your Member of Congress to get involved in an electricity rate case, or local zoning issue, expect to be referred to the state or local government. Some Members may choose to become involved in local issues due to their personal interest in the welfare of the community. Involvement in local issues by Members of Congress is pretty rare, however, and is generally met with some resistance on the part of local officials.

Issues Relating to Other Branches of Government

As noted above, legislators can certainly help you in your interactions with other branches of government. They can send letters, set up meetings and help you sort through the "red tape" of a bureaucracy. However, as we learned in Chapter 3, legislators do not write the regulations that determine how new and existing federal or state programs will be implemented. As a result, they cannot unilaterally change those regulations. While it is entirely appropriate to let your legislator know that you oppose a certain action taking place in an agency, be sure you send a similar letter to the agency, as well as the President (in the case of the federal government) or Governor (in the case of the state government). At the local level, you should also write to the mayor or whoever serves in the "executive branch" capacity.

★ Relationship Building Asks

Despite all the wonderful things your elected officials can do for you, sometimes a hard policy ask isn't quite appropriate. For example, you may be dealing with an elected official you've never talked to before or one that hasn't always been on your side of the issue. Or you might not be ready with a specific policy ask, but you want to be ready to approach the elected official when it's time. This is where a "relationship building ask" comes in handy.

I define a "relationship building ask" as an easy ask or a "soft" ask. It's something you ask for when what you really want to do is "educate" an elected official, but you don't want to tell them that's what you're doing. Often, a "relationship building ask" is something that will provide as much benefit to the elected official as it will to you.

Frankly, the best way to explain a relationship building ask is to provide some examples, such as:

■ **Site Visit:** Asking your elected officials to visit your office, facility, group, site or anything in the area they represent really helps generate enthusiasm for your cause. So, if you're thinking about asking your elected official to support a park, first ask him or her on a short visit to the area you want to turn into a park. If you think that at some point you might ask your state legislator to provide more funds for your local library, start by asking her to visit the library and see for herself how desperately the funds are needed. A site visit is an ideal "ask" because it gives the legislator something easy to say "yes" to. He or she may not yet know whether to spend money on a library, but it's sure hard to say "no" to a simple visit. And then, when it comes time to make the "hard" policy ask, you will already have a positive relationship with the legislator. He or she will (hopefully) be more likely to support you.

- **Community Meeting:** If you don't have a "site" to visit, consider asking your legislators to join you for a community meeting. If you can gather 10 to 20 like-minded constituents of an elected official in one room, he or she will almost always be willing to either attend personally or send a staff person.

- **Write an article for your newsletter:** For advocates affiliated with a state or community organization that puts together a newsletter, asking your elected officials to write an article for that newsletter can be a great way of getting their attention. Most elected officials welcome the opportunity to put their name in front of their constituents, and your request that they post something in your publication will require them to think about your cause. In addition, if they agree to write the article (or, in most cases, to review the article you have drafted for them and agree to sign their name to it) they will almost always want to speak positively about your issue. That makes it much harder for them to vote against you should the time ever come.

- **Make a public statement in support of our cause:** Finally, I have some shocking information for you. Politicians like to talk. So give them something useful to talk about! Ask them to make a statement in any appropriate forum in favor of your cause or provide them with some talking points. Who knows? They might just agree to do so.

The details of how to do all this -- i.e., how to put together a site visit, a community meeting or structuring an article or public statement -- are covered in subsequent chapters. For now, the key point is that it's essential to make an ask, even if the ask is a relatively soft "relationship building" ask. Take a few moments to consider what you want to ask for – next we'll start looking at who you'll be asking.

Chapter 3 (The Not-Too-Boring Structure of Government) hopefully made it clear that there are three different levels of government (local, state and federal) as well as three different branches of government (judicial, executive and legislative). In Chapter 4, we considered the kinds of things elected officials (the legislative branch) can do for you. We focused on the legislative branch because,  believe it or not, it is the most responsive to citizens (or should be). Now, we'll combine that information to help you figure out which audience you should approach with your specific ask.

Why is this important? Shouldn't you just be able to send a letter or make a phone call and be done with it? Well, I might surprise you when I say "absolutely!" See, that's the beauty of citizen advocacy. You can do as much or as little as you want. However, remember that you'll get as much out of it as you put in to it. If you simply want to share your views, aren't too concerned about getting a response and can rest comfortably with the outcome, that's terrific. There's nothing wrong at all with this level of communication and the chapters on putting together an effective letter, meeting or phone call will be very helpful to you. You probably don't need to spend a great deal of time learning about your government.

However, if you're someone that really yearns to make a difference: someone seeking to right wrongs, protect the downtrodden and bring about your version of world peace, you're going to need to take your advocacy to another level. And that's why it's important that you learn more about your audience. After all, you wouldn't ask a car mechanic for advice on your tax return, would you? Then why would you ask a member of the state legislature to help you with a problem at the local or federal level? Or ask a member of any legislature to solve a problem that is strictly an executive or judicial branch matter? OK, granted, it's not exactly like asking your mechanic to help you out on your tax return because, as we noted earlier, the various branches and levels of government do sometimes interact. That said, it is almost always best to build your advocacy effort around the venue or audience most likely to be able to help out.

So, how do you figure that out? Once you've got a general sense of what you want, you'll have to ask yourself some key questions to drill down to the level and branch of government to approach. Those questions are:

- Who does this impact?
- What is the nature of my request?
- Who can really help me get what I want?

Let's look at each in more detail:

⭐ Who Does this Impact?

The first question to ask yourself is who will be impacted by your proposal. Will it be people or businesses in your community, city or county? Will it be people or businesses in two or more cities in your area or the entire state? Will it be people all around the country? It seems like that would be easy to figure out, but it's not always so clear, right? Imagine you were advocating for a new park in your community. You'd like to have a nearby place for your kids to safely play. A small, local park would likely impact just the people in your neighborhood. Your local city council member would be a good place to get the ball rolling.

But what if you want a larger park, perhaps something that requires the protection of a large tract of land? You envision people from all over the region or perhaps even the state coming to enjoy picnics, hikes and whatever natural wonders your park has to offer. You'd probably want to approach your state legislator for something of this scale.

Suppose, though, the park you're envisioning would actually cross state lines. It's not so impossible. Just look at places like the Grand Canyon, Yosemite and the Columbia Gorge National Scenic Area. Or, what if you're eager to protect very large amounts of acreage, or acreage that is in use by the federal government for other purposes (such as timber)? In this scenario, you'd want to approach your federal representatives as the feds would have jurisdiction over anything that crosses state lines or affects existing federal property.

Who knew that the simple act of advocating for a park could be so complicated? But don't worry, if you start by asking yourself "who will be impacted by my proposal", you'll quickly narrow down the best level of government to start with. The next step is to identify the proper branch of government, specifically judicial, executive or legislative. You do that through the next question, "what is the nature of my request?"

★ What is the Nature of My Request?

OK, I know that sounds very Zen, and I don't mean to throw one of those "what is the sound of one hand clapping" riddles at you. The purpose of this question is to help you figure out which branch has jurisdiction over what you want to have happen. Recall from Chapter 3 that the legislative branch makes the laws, the executive branch implements the laws and the judicial branch interprets the laws. So you'll need to figure out whether you want to change the law, change how the law is being implemented or change how the law is being interpreted. Let's look at our park example to demonstrate:

The advocate for a local community park needs to know a little about how parks are approved in his or her neighborhood. In some cases, the city council (i.e., the legislative branch) has a say in designating parks while, in other cases, the local parks department (i.e, the executive branch) holds all the power. Rarely will the judicial branch get involved unless there is a dispute over whether someone thought a park had been legally established or not. So, in this case, the advocate should contact the legislative branch and the executive branch with one simple question, "How are parks established in our neighborhood?" In fact, this question can often be answered over the Internet.

If you're the advocate for a state park you might find yourself in a similar situation. Your state legislature will almost certainly play a role in designating specific areas of land as official state park land while your state Department of Parks and Recreation will actually run the park. Again, the judicial branch is not likely to be involved unless there are legal questions about the designation and/or use of the park. The effective advocate will reach out to both the legislative and executive branches with the question, "How are parks established in our state?" and proceed from there.

At the federal level, the U.S. Congress designates certain lands as federal park land and the U.S. Department of the Interior's National Parks Service administers that land. The U.S. Court System becomes involved only if there are legal questions, such as who actually owns the land or whether this should truly be viewed as a "national" (i.e., not state or local) park. Questions relating to designating a certain area as a "national park" would best be directed to the U.S. House Representative for the area, the two U.S. Senators for the State as well as the National Parks Service.

✪ That's Great, But Who Can Really Help Me?

It probably seems like a lot of work to contact all the potentially relevant legislative and executive branch employees and agencies. I mean, geez, you just want to figure out how parks are established in your area. Isn't there a one-stop shop?

The simple answer is yes, there is – sort of. As your duly elected representatives to the government, your legislators (i.e., members of the legislative branch, like city council members, state legislators and federal legislators) are usually the most appropriate people to help you figure out how the rest of government works. However, with the crush of communications coming in to a legislator's office, your requests for information might not get the attention they deserve. That's why the effective advocate will undertake some of this research on their own. But if you don't have even the slightest idea who can best help you with your issue, start by asking your legislators if they can, at a minimum, point you in the right direction.

Once you've figured out your audience, you'll have to learn a little about the political environment before moving forward. Answer the following questions and you'll be on your way:

- Who are the players?
- How did they get in to power?
- What is the process?
- What's the fiscal situation?
- What's the social situation?

Let's look at each in more detail.

✪ Who are the Players?

Once you've identified your, for lack of a better word, "target" audience, the very first thing you'll want to do is get the names, addresses, e-mails, phone numbers and basic biographical information about the key players. So, if you know that you'll need to approach both the City Council and the local Parks Department, you'll want to create a list of all the city council members, the specifics

on the areas they represent and their contact information. If you're dealing with the state legislature and state parks department or the U.S. Congress and National Parks Service, you'll need to get a list of all those individuals.

You should think of these individuals as your primary audience. In Chapter 6, you'll discover other useful things you'll want to know about them, but for now, just put together a list.

✪ How did they get into Power?

The next thing you'll need to know about these folks is how they got in to power. Basically, you'll need to know if they are elected or appointed. If elected, by who? What group of people do they represent? If appointed, who appoints them? What is the process by which they got in to office?

Looking at the U.S. House of Representatives, for example, you'll discover that every Member of the House represents a specific geographic area called a Congressional district. They got in to office because a majority of people in that Congressional district voted for them. As a result, he or she is responsible to the people in that district. The head of an executive branch agency like the National Parks Service, on the other hand, is often appointed. He will be responsible to the people that appoint him.

Take a minute to review your list of the "players" (your primary audience) and make notes about how they became a player and who might influence them. Consider that list of who might influence the key players your secondary audience.

⊠ What is the Process?

Those advocates who know the rules of the game will have far more success in their advocacy efforts than those who don't. If, for example, you know that the rules of a legislative organization require all bills to be proposed by a certain date, you're going to make sure your favorite initiative gets introduced, right? Or if you know that an executive branch agency must incorporate a public hearing into its decision making process, then you'll be able to point out (politely, if possible, through the courts, if necessary) when those requirements aren't being fulfilled.

Take a little time to learn how decisions are made within the arena in which you'll be advocating. Chapter 3 on The Not-At-All Boring Structure of Government might help. Your research into the key players will help as well. One terrific website that provides "one-stop shopping" for a wealth of information about government at all levels is www.usa.gov.

⊠ What is the Fiscal Situation?

You'll have a lot more difficult time getting money out of your elected officials during an economic downturn than you will when the economy is thriving. That sounds so simple, but you'll be surprised how often we forget to connect the general economic climate with what governments have available to spend. Often, governments are hit with a triple-whammy: first, people lose their jobs so  income tax revenues are lower, then people spend less on consumer goods so sales taxes are lower and, finally, property values plummet resulting in lower property tax revenue.

No, I'm not asking you to feel sorry for those poor governments. Just recognize that much of what you're asking elected officials to do will cost money, whether it's supporting a new park, installing a stop light, increasing funding for your favorite program, decreasing a tax that impacts your business, or changing a regulation. Sometimes we forget that governments do not have an unlimited amount of money to spend: in fact, sometimes governments forget that as well!

Your understanding of the fiscal situation will help you figure out what might be appropriate to ask for as well as how much work you'll have to do to convince your audience that what you want is a good investment.

✪ What is the Social Situation?

Are you in a very conservative area? A very liberal area? Are the demographics of your community older? Younger? Do you have non-native English speakers in your area? Soccer moms? Stay at home dads? Families? Singles? The answer to any of these questions might help you understand how your issue is likely to be perceived.

✪ Pulling it all Together

By answering the questions outlined above, you'll have a better sense of who specifically to approach as well as what avenues might work best to get their attention. You'll also be able to begin to assess whether what you're asking for is even feasbile given your area's fiscal and social environment. Now you're ready to get in to the "nitty gritty" of who's who in a policymaker's office. These are the people you'll soon be bravely calling, writing, e-mailing, meeting or sending smoke signals to very soon.

Congratulations! Now that you've figured out what you want and a little bit about the overall political environment, it's time to delve in to the specifics about the policymakers you'll be approaching. This chapter of the handbook outlines the key questions you'll want to answer about your audience, including:

- What is the policymaker's record on the issues I care about?
- What issues does the policymaker care most about?
- What committees and subcommittees does the policymaker serve on?
- Where is he or she on the seniority scale?
- What party does he or she belong to?
- Does he or she have staff and, if so, how can I best interact with them?

The final section of this chapter offers insights into where you can find these answers. A variety of print, online and phone resources are provided to help you with your research. In addition, you'll find a "legislator profile worksheet" to help you keep track of all the information you've gathered.

★ What You Need to Know: Six Key Questions

Now we'll look in more detail at the six questions outlined above and why they are so critical to advocacy success. Details on how and where to find answers to these questions can be found in the section titled "Where do I Find This Out?" below.

What is the Policymaker's Record on the Issues I Care About?

Most policymakers have a record reflected through one of a variety of ways, including:

- Votes (whether on legislation or regulatory initiatives)
- Formal support of legislation that has been introduced by other policymakers (called cosponsoring a bill)
- Legislation they have introduced themselves (called sponsoring a bill)

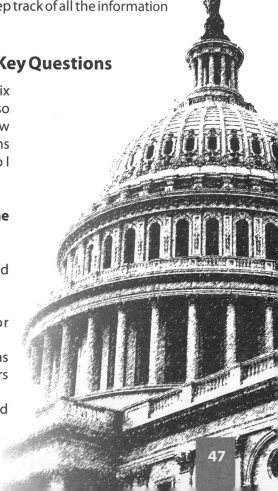

■   Public statements during debates or hearings

Before sending a letter, calling, or asking for a visit, know if your policymaker has a stand on your issues, or, if you're working with an organization, their issues. Knowing this helps you prepare more appropriately for the meeting. For example, you can be prepared to say "thank you" for their past support – or prepare for an energetic discussion about the pros and cons of your policy ask.

What Issues Does the Policymaker Care Most About?
It is also important to know what issues the officials you'll be approaching care passionately about. Being able to present your views in terms your audience understands and agrees with will help you get the most out of your interaction with the office.

In general, policymakers will show their support for a particular issue by sponsoring initiatives or legislation. Before contacting them, know what bills they've introduced – and whether you can connect with them on those issues.

The following scenarios show how this understanding can be used in the real world of meeting with policymakers:

■   **Scenario One:** You are meeting with a member of the state legislature to discuss your support for libraries. In conducting your research, you know that the legislator is very interested in technology issues. Armed with this information, you can tailor your message to focus on the technology libraries provide to the community and gain his or her support for additional funding.

■   **Scenario Two:** A Member of the U.S. Senate has introduced legislation to provide more tax credits for small business. You have scheduled a meeting to discuss a needed change to federal policy that would reduce the reporting burdens on your company. Although this is not exactly a tax credit issue, you can raise your knowledge of the legislator's interest in helping small business and demonstrate how it connects to the policy you've come to discuss.

■   **Scenario Three:** You're meeting with a regulator to discuss your concern about the lack of oversight on a particular regulatory matter. Having done your homework, you know that the regulator has expressed oversight concerns about an unrelated issue. You can connect these concerns by suggesting that the overall issue of "oversight" is a problem. This approach has more potential to capture the regulator's attention and may make him or her more sympathetic to your cause.

What Committee or Committees Is My Member On?

Most legislative branch organizations, whether local, state or federal-based, have committees.[1] Policymakers are assigned to committees based on their interests, their districts (or states, in the case of the U.S. Senate), and, for the more competitive major committees, on how long they have served (seniority). Depending on the level of government, policymakers usually serve on one to three committees and their ability to influence legislation depends largely upon whether they are members of the committee of jurisdiction.[2]

State legislatures vary, but, in general, members of the committee of jurisdiction will have more influence over the policy issues within their committee's jurisdiction.

Knowing the committee assignments of your policymakers can give you insights into the issues that interest him or her and into how he or she will be most effective in helping you with your concern.

Where Is He or She on the Seniority Scale?

At the federal level, and for states without term limits, seniority (or, how long someone has been in office) can be a major factor in determining how much that policymaker can achieve. If your representative is relatively new to office, the unfortunate fact is that he or she is not going to be able to move as many legislative initiatives or secure as many appropriations dollars as a more senior member might be able to do. However, if your member is a Committee Chair or Ranking Member or a member of the leadership, you're in luck. These individuals have a great ability to move policy proposals through the legislative process.

---

[1] Many executive branch organizations have a similar construct, under which employees are assigned to specific divisions or agencies. In addition, executive branch agencies also frequently form informal and formal "working groups" to address a range of policy issues.

[2] This is especially true for the U.S. House, where the structure for consideration of bills can leave little room to change a bill on the floor. In the U.S. Senate, there is often more flexibility for individual senators to make changes when the entire Senate is considering a bill.

What Party Does He or She Belong To?

Policymakers help all constituents, not just those who are affiliated with their political party (as some people believe). After all, your representative has been elected to represent you and your interests, regardless of your party affiliation. But it is important to know the member's party affiliation to determine if they are part of

the majority or minority party in the legislature. While many policymakers seek to work collaboratively and across party lines, those of the majority party still have an advantage in efforts to get legislative proposals passed.

Does He or She Have Staff? How do I Interact with Them?

Understanding the structure of a policymaker's office is key to successfully communicating your views and influencing action. Many local councils, state legislatures and the U.S. Congress have staff people who serve either specific elected officials or the organization as a whole. Never feel that it's a waste of time to meet with "just staff." In fact, these individuals can be instrumental in addressing your concerns.

In this section, you will learn "who's who" in a policymaker's office and how to work with them. We'll look at the federal staffing structure for the U.S. Congress as well as sample state level constructs. Specifics about how meetings are scheduled, how phone calls are handled, and how mail is answered are outlined in subsequent sections.

What's Missing?

Sometimes people wonder whether it's important to know who contributed to an elected official's campaign. While this type of information may be interesting (and is accessible via a site like opensecrets.org), it is not always as illuminating as one might think and, unfortunately, sometime leads to cynicism.

The truth is that political contributions can provide insights into the types of interests in an elected official's district. For example, a contribution from a large business may indicate that business is headquartered in the district or has a large number of employees there. Likewise, a contribution from a special interest group might suggest that there is a large number of members of that group in the district. And in most cases, elected officials will actually support or oppose certain positions as a result of the district connection, not the campaign contribution.

Regardless of how you feel about money in the political process (and most of us are feeling pretty skeptical), recall that the most important power anyone has with an elected official is their power of constituency – and that's an important tool to help you get your foot in the door! If you want to contribute to the campaign of an elected official, do it because you think he or she already understands your issue or is willing to learn – NOT because you think it will buy you a vote or access. Likewise, if you're considering becoming a contributing member of your organization's PAC (which you should), do so as part of the organization's long-term policy and legislative campaign, not because you think it's the only way to get attention.

★ Federal Level

District/State vs. Washington, D.C., Staff

Members of Congress have at least two offices, one in Washington, D.C., and one or more in their district or state. House Members usually have one or two district offices, depending upon the geographical area they serve. Senate offices generally have two to five offices within the state, some of which may be staffed by only one person. Each office has a number of staff people with various responsibilities. The average House Member has a total of 14 staff people (in D.C. and the district). In the Senate, the amount of funding available for staff positions varies depending on the population of the state. Senators from less populated states have an average of 31 staffers, while senators from more-populated states have an average of 44. Communicating effectively with your representatives can hinge on reaching the right staff person.

Representatives and senators can structure their offices however they see fit. There are no formal rules about staff roles or titles. What follows is a breakdown of the traditional roles and titles of key staff members you are likely to find in most district/state and D.C. policymaker's offices.

District/State Staff

The district/state office is a good first point of contact for most constituents. House Members generally have from six to eight people located in the district. Senators usually have 10 to 15 staffers located in the state.

■ ***Caseworkers*** -- If you are looking for help on a problem concerning federal agencies (such as getting your social security check) ask for the caseworker who handles that issue (the social security caseworker, for example). District or state caseworkers are masters at maneuvering through the maze of the federal bureaucracy. Their expertise ranges from immigration to social security to veteran's benefits, and they spend most of their time solving the problems constituents encounter with the federal government. For example, a district/state caseworker can help you secure your veteran's benefits, or resolve immigration issues.

■ ***District/State Scheduler*** -- If you want to meet with the representative or senator in the district or state, or if you want to invite him/her to an event, ask for the district or state scheduler. This is the person who schedules the Member's time when he or she is in the district or state. (Note that some offices handle all scheduling out of one office, usually the D.C. office, so you may be referred to the D.C. scheduler). Senate offices may have more than one person per office dealing with scheduling duties.

■ ***Field Representative*** -- If you want to meet with a district staff person to discuss a particular local issue, or if you want to invite someone from the district staff to a local event or meeting, ask for the field representative who handles your issue. Field representatives can also talk with you about federal issues that directly affect the district (disaster relief for your flooded neighborhood, for example) or actions of a federal agency on something that affects a local group of people or a community (as opposed to individual problems).

■ ***District/State Office Director*** -- This staffer oversees the operations of the district or state staff and is often the point person in the district office for highly sensitive local political issues. Constituents should ask for this person if they feel that their concerns are not being met by others in the office.

Washington, D.C., Staff

Washington, D.C., staff are less focused on casework and specific local issues and more focused on legislation. They are ready and willing to answer constituent's questions about specific legislative proposals. In general, if you want to express your opinion or learn the Member's opinion on a particular federal issue that is broad in scope, call or write the Washington, D.C. office. You can also contact the district office, but in many cases your correspondence will be forwarded to Washington.

- **Staff Assistant** -- Most House offices have one staff assistant. Most Senate offices have at least two. They handle the front desk duties, which include answering phones, greeting visitors, sorting mail, and coordinating tours. In many offices, these individuals will handle a few policy issues as well. If you are going to be traveling to Washington and want tickets to tour a government building, be sure to ask for the staff assistant/tours coordinator (in a few offices, these are different people), who can let you know what's available. Be sure to plan ahead for such requests, since tickets for some of the more popular tours are claimed months in advance, and each policymaker's office receives a limited supply. Buildings where tours are available include the Capitol, the White House, FBI headquarters, the Bureau of Engraving and Printing, the Kennedy Center, and the Supreme Court. (In most cases, you can still tour these buildings without passes from your policymaker's office ahead of time, but you may have to wait in long lines.) You can also receive passes to view House and Senate floor debates.

- **D.C. Scheduler/Executive Assistant** -- If you are going to be in Washington, D.C and want to meet your representative or senator, contact the D.C. scheduler (who is sometimes called the Executive Assistant). Information on effective meetings is outlined in following chapters -- but here's the first rule: Do not be surprised or insulted if your representative or senator does not have time for a meeting. Schedulers receive dozens of meeting requests a day. Most House Members are scheduled with back-to-back meetings and votes from about 8 am to 9 or 10 pm every weekday, and also have four to five hours of meetings both weekend days. There simply is not enough time in the day for a Member of Congress to meet with everyone who requests a meeting. That said, if you live in the district or state that the representative or senator represents, and want to discuss a substantive policy issue, you always should be able to meet with someone on the staff. In fact, as noted below, meeting with the staff may, in many ways, be even more effective.

- **Legislative Assistant (LA)** -- If you want to talk, either in person or on the phone, about a particular policy issue, ask for the legislative assistant who handles that issue. Legislative assistants handle the bulk of the policy work in a policymaker's office. A House office usually will have two to four LAs and a Senate office will have from three to as many as 12 (depending upon the state's population).

- *Legislative Director (LD)* -- In some cases, the person who handles your issue may also be the legislative director who, in addition to handling policy issues, also oversees the legislative staff. There is usually just one legislative director in each policymaker's office.

- *Legislative Correspondent(LC)* -- You may also be referred to a legislative correspondent who, in addition to drafting letters in response to constituents' comments and questions, also generally handles a few legislative issues. Most House offices have one or two LC's. Senators have three to five, depending on their state's population.

- *Press Secretary/Spokesperson/Communications Director* -- Press Secretary/Spokesperson/Communications Director -- If you want to include something about the representative or senator's views in a newsletter, or have questions related to the press operations of the office, ask for the press secretary. This individual is responsible for fielding all calls from the media and is often the spokesperson for the office. House offices usually have one designated press person. Senate offices have two to five.

- **Chief of Staff (CoS)/Administrative Assistant (AA)** -- The chief of staff or AA oversees the entire operation. The chief of staff may sometimes handle a few policy issues, but generally his or her time is spent managing the office.

✪ State Level Constructs

Every state legislature differs in terms of staff. Some have as many as 3,000, while others have under 100.[3] Some serve only during the legislative session, others have permanent staff. In some cases, individual members of the House / Senate are authorized to hire staff; in others all the staff are centralized. Following are a few of the different constructs for legislative staff in the various states[4].

- *Individual Staff Hired by Each Legislator:* Some states (like California and Oregon) authorize members to hire their own staff both in the Capitol and the district. These individuals serve specific members and/or legislative districts, much like the federal level construct. Titles range from Chief of Staff to Legislative Assistant.

---

[3]For information on staff counts, see the National Conference of State Legislatures site at http://www.ncsl.org/programs/legismgt/about/staffcount2003.htm
[4]A full profile of staff in all 50 states is available at http://www.ncsl.org/programs/legismgt/about/sdoverview.htm (click on "profiles")

- *Individual Staff Hired by the Organization and Assigned to Legislators:* Some states hire a pool of nonpartisan legislative staff who may be assigned to one or more members of the legislature. They may perform administrative and scheduling duties, respond to constituents or assist in moving legislative initiatives.

- *Leadership Staff:* Most legislatures allow leadership to hire their own staff. These individuals tend to be either partisan staffers devoted to moving the legislative agenda of the party or nonpartisan staff dedicated to the proper functioning of the legislative body.

- *Shared Staff:* Most legislatures have some sort of shared staffing structure for overall services of the legislature, such as Committee staff, bill drafting or budget analysis. These individuals are not connected with a particular member.

- *Session Only vs. Permanent:* Another important distinction between state-level staff constructs and the federal level is that some legislatures have only a limited number of permanent staff and increase their staff during the legislative session to provide assistance to individual representatives. Texas, for example, has approximately 1,700 permanent staff and hires another 500+ during the legislative session.

- *Non-staff Legislatures:* There are no legislatures that have absolutely no staff, but there are several that have only a small pool of staff that are not associated with individual members and perform only basic day-to-day operations functions of the legislature.

⭐ Tips on Working with Staff

Regardless of whether you're dealing with federal staff, state staff or even local staff, following are some tips for working with these hard-working individuals:

- *Staff Contact Has Advantages Over Member Contact* -- First and foremost, recognize that meeting with a staff person, rather than directly with the policymaker, is often to your advantage. Staff can take a little more time to delve in to a particular issue and gain a greater understanding of why what you're

proposing is such a great idea. With a little work on your part, they can become advocates for your cause within the policymaker's office. A great deal of what actually gets done, whether it's an appropriation for a particular project or a change in law to help your export business, is done through the initiative and sweat of the staff, so never feel like your communications with them are a waste of time. Having the ear of a staffer who likes your issue, wants to work on it, and, most important, wants his or her boss to spend time on it, can only help your cause.

■ *Talk to the Right Person* -- Many people are under the mistaken impression that they should always try to communicate with the most senior staff person (for example, the LD or the AA at the federal level) in a policymaker's office. While having a positive relationship with senior staff can be helpful, it is best to communicate with the person in the office who handles the issues you care about, no matter what their position in the office. In most cases, when you call senior staff to request a meeting on a particular issue, you will simply be directed to the person who has responsibility for that issue. This is the individual who will provide advice to the member and senior staff on voting, bill cosponsorships, and letter sign-ons. By starting with that person, you save yourself a step and the irritating feeling of being passed around. It will also avoid any conflict with that person about the perception that you may be "going over their head" to get something done.

There are three exceptions to this rule. First, it is always okay to contact senior staff if you're not sure who to contact and the staff assistant cannot direct you to the right person. Second, in situations where more than one person can have responsibility for specific issues, it does make sense to contact the more senior individual as that person will generally have more access to the policymaker. Third, if your request is of a highly political or sensitive nature, or if it is campaign-related, you should feel free to contact a senior staff person, who will be able to provide advice and point you in the right direction.

■ *Remember, Your Issue Is One of Many* -- Staff handle a bewildering array of issues. They simply cannot know about everything related to any of their issue areas. This is especially true for issues that are not directly related to the member's committee or legislative agenda. The purpose of any meeting with a policymaker's staff and/or the member should be to share with them your views on issues you care about. If they aren't familiar with the issue, take that as a perfect opportunity to bring them up to speed!

Issue assignments in policymakers' offices are generally based on what individual staff people are interested in and what they are knowledgeable about. Because someone is assigned a particular issue, however, does not mean that they are experts. Generally, environmental LAs do not have degrees in ecology, health care LAs are not doctors, transportation LAs are not traffic engineers, and science LAs are not physicists[5]. Rather, the issue area assignments help designate for the outside world who the ecologists, doctors, traffic engineers and physicists should talk with about particular policy proposals. The staff person's job is to sift through this bewildering array of information, much of it contradictory, to provide advice to the Member on the policy issues for which that staff person is responsible.

- *Institutional Memory in a Policymaker's Office Can Be Short* -- Because of the wide-array of issues and high staff turnover, you may sometimes be surprised to find entirely new people working on your issues. Depending upon the office, these turnovers can happen once every few months to once every couple years. The point is that it is rare to find the same staffer working on a particular issue in a member's office for longer than two years or so. When there is staff turnover, you will need to impart the history of your relationship with the office and your background in the policy issue. Be prepared to do so quickly and to supply supporting materials.

- *Expect (and Appreciate) Youth* -- Most staffers are young, 25 or younger. The person you're meeting with may not look as if he or she is old enough to vote! Don't let that throw you. In most cases, staffers are bright and capable individuals who can be trusted to respond appropriately to your requests and deliver your message to your representative or senator.

★ Where Can I Find All This Out?

By now, you hopefully recognize the value of doing some research on policymakers before approaching them. But where do you find the answers? The following resources should help. In general, to be most effective your approach should be to find out as much information as you can on your own using the wealth of information available on the Internet, at your library or by contacting your elected official's office.

Your Organization's Website or Government Relations Office

Assuming you're undertaking this advocacy effort in coordination with a national, state or local level organization, such as an association or a corporation, the first stop for finding out this information should be the organization itself. In some cases, your organization will have an online advocacy center on its website that you can use to

---

[5]Note, however, that some professional associations do offer internships that serve to match these types of professionals with a policymaker's office over the course of a few months or a year. The American Planning Association, for example, offers a Capitol Hill fellowship that places professional urban planners in the offices of Members of Congress.

figure out who your legislators are, what committees they are on, what bills they've introduced, their party affiliation and the names of their key staff.

In addition, some organizations provide highlights on how policymakers have voted on key issues. Some even create "scorecards" for this purpose. Finally, as mentioned in earlier chapters, your organization's website will often provide detailed information on the policy asks.

It's always a good idea to check your organization's website to see if this information is available. If you can't find it on the site, you may be able to answer your questions through the additional resources noted below, or you can check in with the government relations staff of your organization to see if they can help point you in the right direction.

That said, don't be surprised if the government relations staff do not yet know much about a specific policymaker's views on your organization's issues. In some cases, there may be no real legislative or regulatory history on an issue. In others, policymakers may not yet have formed an opinion about the issue. In still others, policymakers may have been unwilling to share their views with the organization: in fact, they are far more likely to share their views with you, the actual constituent, which is why your participation is so critical.

Other Online Research Sources
Following is a small selection of the thousands of websites that can provide you with the information you need to answer the questions noted above. These are commonly used, reliable and nonpartisan sites.

- **Congress.org:** This site, made available through Capitol Advantage, a leading provider of online advocacy tools, allows users to look up biographical, committee, staff and other critical information about their elected officials at the state and federal levels. In addition, users can send communications through the site, start petitions and post their views on every issue under the sun.

- **Thomas.gov:** The "Thomas" website, maintained by the Library of Congress, provides up-to-date information on Congressional activities. It is the ideal place to look for information on legislation that your elected officials have introduced in order to get a better sense of what issues interest them most. In addition, you can review the Congressional Record, which chronicles the daily activities of the U.S. Congress. Members of Congress often submit statements about issues they care about in the record. You can review the statements your elected officials have made on the issues that matter most to you.

- **Congressional Research Service Reports:** The Congressional Research Service has a helpful guide for tracking legislation and federal agency actions called "Tracking Current Federal Legislation and Regulations: A Guide to Resources." You can find it, and many other CRS reports, on the House Rules Committee website at http://www.rules.house.gov/CRS_Rpt/index.html. The link for this specific report is http://www.rules.house.gov/CRS_Rpt/RL33895.pdf

- **VoteSmart.org:** The Vote Smart site allows you to search for votes based on a topic, and covers both the U.S. House and Senate as well as state offices. It also supplies basic biographical information about elected officials and candidates, links to public statements and speeches, interest group ratings and campaign finance information.

- **USA.gov:** USA.gov is a site maintained by the Federal Government, designed as a "one-stop shop" for information about government services. Information is structured by audience (for example, "for citizens" or "for business") and provides links to a wealth of information at both the state and federal level.

- **House.gov and Senate.gov:** These are the websites of the U.S. House of Representatives and U.S. Senate, respectively. Here, you can gain access to the websites of individual Members of Congress, which will tell you a great deal about their priorities and background. You can also learn about the various committees and, through a review of committee jurisdictions, identify the names of the committees most relevant to your specific issue.

- **National Conference of State Legislatures:** Gain access to the legislative websites for each of the 50 states at the National Conference of State Legislatures state website look-up page at http://www.ncsl.org/public/leglinks.cfm. Once you've found the sites for your state, in many cases (depending on the information made available by your state) you can gain access to the critical information you might need about your state legislators.

Outside Interest Groups

Interest groups can be a good source of some basic information about how policymakers vote. Bear in mind, however, that such groups' presentation of voting records can be colored by their views and the views of their leadership. Many of these organizations will choose only about 20 votes to rate in a given year (out of 400 to 500). These votes are selected to reflect the group's agenda and views. For example, the League of Conservation Voters focuses on a few important environmental votes. Lawmakers that are more "green" by the LCV's standards will get much higher scores. The American Conservative Union focuses on what it considers to be critical conservative votes, with the more conservative lawmakers coming across favorably.

Here's a smattering of individual sites and the types of voting records they reflect:

- www.lcv.org
  (League of Conservation Voters -- environment voting records)
- www.ntu.org
  (National Taxpayers Union -- taxpayer / government waste voting records)
- www.nfib.org
  (National Federation of Independent Businesses -- small business voting records)
- www.acu.org
  (American Conservative Union -- conservative voting records)
- www.ada.org
  (Americans for Democratic Action -- liberal voting records)

Book / Print Resources

Numerous publications provide a range of information about legislators and the legislative districts they serve. Many can be found through online resources or at your local bookstore or library. They include:

- Almanac of American Politics
- Original U.S. Congress Handbook
- Almanac of the Unelected
- Leadership Directories Yellow Book

The Policymaker's Office

Finally, it is always appropriate to contact a policymaker's office and ask if he or she is a cosponsor of particular legislation, or how he or she voted on a particular issue. However, this is not the quickest way to get information, as your request will most likely be passed on to the office's legislative correspondent, who will have to draft a written response to your question. Because the LC must respond to upwards of 100,000 requests in a year, it may be weeks before you receive a response. A little research on your own can often generate faster answers.

⭐ Legislator Profile Worksheet

What do you do with all this information once you have it? Try using this handy-dandy legislator profile form to help you capture all the detailed information you need about the elected officials who represent you (you can also adapt this tool to learn about any regulators that may impact your life!).

LEGISLATOR PROFILE WORKSHEET

Name of Legislator:_____

Address: _____

City: _____ State: _____ Zip: _____

Phone: _____ E-mail:_____

Website: _____ District / Party: _____

Name of staff person handling your issues:

_____

Is this a new legislator (i.e., new to this particular office):　☐ Yes ☐ No

If known, what are three of his / her top policy interests?

• *Hint: for incumbent U.S. Congress reps check www.congress.gov for previously introduced legislation as well as www.house.gov or www.senate.gov for individual member webpages.*

• *For incumbent State Legislators, check the state legislative websites for previously introduced legislation*

• *You might also try a "Google" search at www.google.com*

1. _____

2. _____

3. _____

If known, please indicate whether this legislator supported or opposed your issues in the past *(Hint: some national associations post "vote ratings". You can also check individual U.S. Congressional votes on www.congress.gov)*

1. _____

2. _____

3. _____

If known, please make notes about any previous contact with this legislator (meetings, phone calls, fundraising, etc.)

_____

_____

Did you support this candidate? ☐ Yes ☐ No ☐ Did Not Know of Candidate

If yes, did you actively support? (i.e., volunteering on his/her campaign, attending a fundraiser, setting up a meeting)   ☐ Yes ☐ No

Do you know this legislator personally?: ☐ Yes ☐ No ☐ Somewhat

Please note any personal connections (i.e., "went to school together", "worked together" etc.)

_____

_____

Please make note of any other relevant information about this legislator:

_____

_____

Would you be willing to contact this legislator in the future? ☐ Yes ☐ No

Your Name: _____

Address: _____

City: _____ State: _____ Zip: _____

Phone: _____ E-mail: _____

In earlier chapters, you've figured out what you want to ask for as well as a little bit about the audience that you'll be approaching. Now it's time to look at developing a message that really resonates. This section provides pointers on how to develop your message so that it will have the most impact.

The most important thing to remember in developing your message is that **you have something of value to contribute.** You probably have a particular reason why you feel the way you do about a specific policy proposal, or a reason why you're seeking a change in law. A thoughtful approach to policy issues combined with a careful explanation of why it's important to you personally is very compelling to policymakers.

One of your main jobs as an effective advocate is to act as a resource for the policymaker. There is no way you are going to be able to relay everything you know about your issues or business in one 15-minute meeting. What you REALLY want to relay is that you know a great deal about the issues you are there to discuss and, in particular, you know a great deal about how those issues impact people in the district or state. Because they must, by necessity, be generalists, policymakers and their staff often turn to trusted outside experts to gain a better understanding. If you are an expert in your field, let your officials know that you are available to answer any questions they may have.

With these important thoughts in mind, in this chapter we'll look at strategies for overall message development, regardless of what technique you'll use (such as phone calls, meetings or written communications) to deliver the message. Specific ideas for the different forms of communication are discussed in subsequent chapters. Our topics for this chapter include:

- Utilizing the results of your research
- The power of personalizing
- Three key elements of winning messages
- A message forumula

⭐ Utilizing the Results of Your Research

As you consider the development of your winning message, think about how you can best utilize the results of the research you've conducted on your audience. For example:

- Because you know what policies the official cares about, you'll be able to talk about your issues in terms he or she understands and can relate to. Or, you can talk about how you might be able to help out on an issue of great concern to the official.

- Because you know more about the official's personal background (where he or she went to school, for example), you can make connections based on non-policy related matters, such as personal hobbies or whether you graduated from the same school.

- Because you know more about the constituency he or she represents, you'll be able to make the issues more relevant by commenting on the direct and specific impacts on the people he or she represents.

- Because you know whether the official has taken a position on your issues in the past, you can thank him or her for past support – or gently guide him or her, through your persuasive arguments, toward a better policy direction.

By demonstrating your understanding of the audience, and tailoring your messages accordingly, you'll have a far greater chance of being heard – and perhaps the official will even agree with you!

⭐ The Power of Personalizing

Every recent report about communicating with elected officials highlights the importance of relevant, thoughtful and, most important, personalized messages. The Congressional Management Foundation, for example, recently conducted a survey of Congressional staff asking what types of messages made an impression with them. One of the most important findings was that personalized communications are extremely powerful.

What does this mean for you? Well, if an organization has asked you to respond to an action alert by sending a communication through their online advocacy center, go ahead and send it. But, if possible, personalize the communication with your own take on the issue. Explain through a short anecdote or story how the policy issue impacts you directly. Officials recognize the time it takes to personalize a message, and will focus their efforts on those communications.

In essence, your goal is to make it real for the policymaker or staff person. They will get all the facts, figures and statistics from any template communications, as well as the national, state or regional organization (where applicable). What you bring to the table is a compelling story about the impact of policy issues on people that the policymaker represents.

You can achieve this goal by telling a personal story. Think about it: there's some reason why you've decided to be an advocate on your issues. It likely impacts you directly in some deeply personal way. That's the message you need to relay to your policymakers.

Here are some questions / ideas to help you develop your personal story:

Why did you become an advocate? How do the issues you are discussing impact you directly?

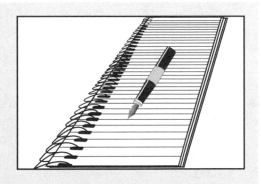

- Do they cost you money?
- Do they impact your health or the health of loved ones?
- Do they conflict with your organization's core mission?
- Do they impact your ability to do your job?

Do you have clients / customers / friends / colleagues that offer a compelling story? Have they:

- Benefited from your services?
- Contributed to your cause?
- Joined your campaign because of their own strong views?

How do these people and others connect to those the policymaker represents?

Take a few minutes to weave these questions into a story / anecdote:

_____

_____

_____

_____

_____

★ Five Key Elements of Effective Messages

As you work to develop your messages, know that truly effective messages contain the following elements:

■ **Relevancy:** Effective messages demonstrate their relevancy to the policymaker in two ways. First, they highlight the impact on those who the official represents by commenting on the impact of a particular policy position on people in the district. Second, they seek to connect the policy issue at hand to an issue or series of issues that the policymaker has expressed interest on in the past.

■ **Specific:** Effective messages are also very specific about what the policymaker can do to help solve a problem. This is essentially the "ask." It may be a policy-related ask, such as "will you cosponsor this bill" or a relationship-building ask, such as "will you visit us in the district?" See Chapter 4 for more information on "asks."

■ **Truthful:** Being absolutely sure of any facts you relay is vital. Policymakers often rely on the expertise of others to help them understand the ramifications of particular policy proposals. If you provide information to an official's office with specifics about how a particular policy will affect you, your business, or your community, you are likely to be taken at your word. If your facts are wrong, you may regret not double-checking them. Of course, it is always OK to be unsure of the implications. Even after you've done your research, the implications of a certain policy proposal may simply be unclear. If you are asked a question you don't know the answer to, the best thing to say is "I don't know, but I'll get back to you" – and then get back to them!

■ **Positive:** Effective messages are "positive" in two ways. First, they focus on the positive steps that can be taken to solve a problem. In other words, they focus on the benefits that a particular action will bring to the community. Second, positive messages stay away from referring to government as "evil" or "wasteful." Even if you think an official has proposed the stupidest and most blatantly wrong-headed policy you've ever encountered, remember that in communicating with policymakers, you are talking to someone who is part of the government. In fact, you are part of the government! Referring to government as evil simply perpetuates the negative cycle. Instead, focus on the actions that can be taken to ensure what you consider to be a good policy outcome.

■ **Brief:** Perhaps most important, effective messages are brief! In some cases, you may have only five minutes to get your message across. Use the time as wisely as possible to relay your key concerns – and what the policymaker can do to help!

✪ Pulling it All Together: The Message Formula

The following formula can be used to help you weave each of these elements in to a winning message. While you want to make every message your own, this formula will help in creating your initial message, which you can "tweak" to suit your own needs and interests.

■ Knowing of your interest in [fill in the blank with something that you know about the policymaker, such as policy issues he or she is passionate about or legislation he or she has introduced]. *Through this step you are demonstrating relevance to the issues the policymaker cares about.*

■ We would like to talk to you about our ideas on [fill in with a specific description of your policy issues]. *Through this step, you are outlining the specific issue you want to discuss, along with the specific ask, where applicable.*

■ We represent [fill in with a number or other quantifiable description] of your constituents. *Through this step you are demonstrating your relevance to those the policymaker represents.*

■ We would like to provide the following benefits to them [fill in with the positive outcomes of your proposed policy]. *Through this step you are demonstrating your positive approach.*

■ To do so, we are seeking [fill in with your "ask"]. *Through this step you are demonstrating the specific action an official can take to help you achieve your goal.*

■ We believe this is important because [fill in with your personal story]. *Through this step you are making the policy issue real for the official.*

■ Closing statement: We hope that you will be a partner with us in providing [list benefits] to the residents of [list community/constituent area] by [specific target]. *Through this step you are summarizing the message.*

✪ Filled Out Message Formula

How does this work? Let's imagine that you were contacting a legislator in support of legislation promoting tax credits for hybrid vehicles. Although the legislator hasn't taken a position on these issues in the past, you know from your research that she is very interested in technology issues. You also know that her district is a suburban district, where people have to drive far and sit in traffic to get to work. Many constituents are also concerned about the environment. Here's how you might use this formula to create a customized message:

■ Knowing of your interest in technology issues...

■ ... we would like to talk to you about our ideas on promoting hybrid fuel technology, specifically, legislation to promote hybrid car tax credits. We believe this legislation may help facilitate a technological solution to some economic and environmental problems in our area.

■ I live in your district and represent thousands of other constituents who must drive long distances and sit in traffic to get to jobs downtown. In addition, air pollution from mobile sources, such as cars, is on the rise.

■ This legislation would provide the following benefits to us:

  ● A tax credit for hybrid cars would save us money, both in terms of potential tax refunds but also in terms of gasoline costs. In addition, with decreased gasoline consumption, we would hope to see improvements in our air quality. Finally, as a result of this tax credit, automakers would be encouraged to build more hybrid cars, increasing the reach of this important technology.

■ To achieve these goals, we are asking you to cosponsor and actively support the legislation.

■ We believe this is important because many of us are being negatively impacted by increases in gasoline prices. Many of us have to make choices between what we might need or want for our family and the sheer reality of filling the tank every couple days. A hybrid car tax credit would provide us with the economic incentive we need to become less reliant on expensive gasoline. In addition, we want to do everything we can to improve air quality in our area. Last summer, for example, we had more "dangerous" air quality days than in previous years, threatening the ability of our children to play outside. We believe this legislation is a step in the right direction for helping achieve these goals for our community.

■ We hope that you will be a partner with us in providing these economic and environmental benefits to the residents of your district by cosponsoring the legislation. We look forward to your response.

★ Conclusion

Believe it or not, what you say to policymakers actually matters! They are far more likely to pay close attention to communications that are specific, personal, relevant, truthful and brief. In this chapter, we've looked at ways to use all the research you've done to craft truly memorable messages. Now it's time to look at how you might want to deliver those messages, as well as some potential pitfalls to avoid. For example, it's rarely effective to say to a legislator "I pay your salary, so you have to do what I say," but if I had a dime for everytime someone said something like that to me when I was working for a member of Congress, well, I wouldn't have needed a government job.

Having taken the time to craft the perfect message, you need to deliver it in a way that will make policymakers and their staff sit up and take notice. This section will help you decide what tool to use (phone, e-mail, letter or meeting), and how to ensure that you make your message stand out among the hundreds that pour into a policymaker's office every day. To help you achieve this goal, this chapter is designed to help you assess the various approaches and offers ten tips for effective message delivery.

★ Method of Communication: Assessing the Approaches

Should you call, e-mail, or seek a meeting with policymakers? The very first thing you should know is that what you say to policymakers is far more important than how you say it. Assuming that you have developed a compelling, thoughtful, truthful and positive message, you are likely to at least be listened to -- and hopefully have an impact -- however you choose to deliver the message.

That said, recent studies have indicated that while all communications from constituents are important, some methods capture slightly more attention. In fact, congressional staff, when asked as part of the Congressional Management Foundation's 2005 report, *Communicating with Congress: How Capitol Hill is Coping with the Surge in Citizen Advocacy*, which advocacy techniques might have the most influence on Members of Congress, rated the various approaches as follows:

1. In-person visits from constituents – 99% found these to be either very influential or somewhat influential
2. Individual postal letters from constituents – 96% found these to be either very influential or somewhat influential
3. Individual e-mail communications from constituents – 94% found these to be either very influential or somewhat influential
4. Individual faxes from constituents – 91% found these to be either very influential or somewhat influential
5. Individual phone calls from constituents –88% found these to be either very influential or somewhat influential

By contrast, form communications, such as form e-mails, postal letters or faxes, ranked at the bottom of the "influence" pyramid, with only between 57 and 65% of the respondents finding that any of these communications were influential at all and the vast majority found these only somewhat influential[1].

Clearly, the overall key for any communication is that it be personalized and relevant. But how do you choose between the range of potentially effective approaches? Consider the following questions to help you decide:

- What does the organization I'm working with recommend or provide? Many organizations offer advocates the ability to send e-mail or fax communications through an online advocacy center. In fact, you may be deciding to advocate on an issue because of an e-mail action alert you've received from a national or state organization. Since these communications, when personalized, can be very influential, this is certainly a great (and often easy) way to deliver your message.

- How complicated is the issue? Is this a simple "vote yes" or "vote no" message or is there more to explain? Some methods of communication are simply better suited to some types of messages than others. For example, a simple request to vote for a particular bill can easily be relayed over the phone, while a more complicated message might better be put in writing.

- Can I take the time or financial investment to visit with my officials either in the capitol or their district offices? As noted above, in-person meetings are hugely influential. But you don't always have to fly out to Washington, D.C. or the state capitol to have an impact. In fact, policymakers have staff available in the areas

---

[1]Congressional Management Foundation, Communicating with Congress: How Capitol Hill is Coping with the Surge in Citizen Advocacy. Available online at www.cmfweb.org

they represent. In addition, the officials themselves often work out of their district offices. Learn more about setting up a district meeting or site visit in Chapter 9, which covers meetings.

■ How do I express myself best? If you express yourself best in writing, write a letter or send an e-mail message[2]. If you want to meet with your representative face-to-face and are confident you have a winning message, seek to set up a meeting, either in D.C. or the district office. If you like talking through the issues, call the office on the phone.

■ What does my audience respond to? Asking one simple question of your policymakers and their staff can make all the difference in getting a response. It's as simple as "how do you prefer I contact your office?" When starting to build a relationship with the key staff as well as the official him or her-self, ask then what method of communication they prefer. Believe me, if you use e-mail to communicate with a phone person or vice-versa, you're going to have a difficult time getting them to even review your comments, much less respond.

In other words, figure out what works best for you personally as well as the message you're delivering. And remember, there's often no need to reinvent the wheel: a national or state organization may be able to help!

✪ Ten Tips for Delivering Effective Messages

Whichever method you choose, following are some overall tips to bear in mind when delivering your advocacy message. Subsequent chapters cover the details of certain delivery approaches, such as phone calls, written communications and meetings.

Tip #1: Volume Does Not Always Equal Effectiveness

Highly controversial issues that are national in scope can create a flurry of phone calls, e-mails, letters, postcards, petitions, faxes, and meetings. It certainly sends a dramatic message when all the phone lines are busy for days at a time, people are swarming in the hallways, the

---

[2]Note, however, that written communications sent through the U.S. Post Office to Capitol Hill in Washington, D.C. must go through an irradiation process that delays the receipt of mail and, in some cases, makes it nearly unreadable when it does arrive. See Chapter 10 for more information.

Capitol servers crash due to the onslaught of e-mails, or an office receives thousands of postcards or form letters. Many offices will tally these communications and consider the numbers when making a decision on a particular action, but only to a point. One thoughtful and well-argued message can have more of an impact than a thousand letters or calls.

The point here is not to discourage people who choose to participate by simply expressing their opinion in a phone call, participating in a postcard campaign, sitting in on a meeting, or signing a petition. Some offices do keep a tally of how many people communicated on a particular topic, which may have some minimal effect on what actions the policymaker decides to take. If you want to simply send a message to officials, and aren't too concerned about receiving a response, these types of activities are fine. However, if you want to get a response, or to have someone in the office think very carefully about the questions you've raised, you'll need to put some time and effort into a more personal, thoughtful message.

If you do decide to communicate through a form or standardized communication, do not be disappointed if the office responds to you in-kind. Too many advocates express their opinion by taking 30 seconds or 1 minute to sign a petition or click on a link to send a form e-mail and then are horrified when they receive a form letter in response!

Tip #2: Always Identify Yourself as a Constituent
It is a waste of your time and money to communicate with your policymakers without making it clear how you are connected to the district or state they represent. Remember that policymakers and their staff are excited to meet you because you are constituents or you represent the concerns of constituents, not necessarily because you are associated with a specific national or state-level organization.

Tip #3: Be Specific
Too often, policymakers receive vague, unspecific comments like "we should pay less in taxes," or "the EPA should stop picking on my business." These types of messages usually receive a very pro-forma response, something along the lines of "gee thanks, I'll keep your views in mind." To be more effective, you must ask officials to do something specific related to your position.

Tip #4: Prioritize Your Requests

If you ask for too many things without making it clear what your top priorities are, the policymaker you're approaching may feel overwhelmed and be unable to identify a few key areas on which to expend limited staff resources. Let the office know what action needs the most attention in the short term. Better yet, try to time your requests so that you are not asking for more than a few things at once.

Tip #5: Don't Vilify Your Opponents

Or, at the very least, you should refrain from labeling those who disagree with you as unenlightened idiots. Try to take it one step further, and grant the credibility of opposing views. If you do so, the policymaker's staff are more likely to believe that you have developed your position based on a careful evaluation of the facts. This is not to say that you shouldn't feel passionately about your position. However, when you insist that the goal of the individuals on the opposite side of the issue is to drive you out of business, policymakers may question whether the facts you have presented are colored by your intense feelings on the issue.

Tip #6: Be Polite

You know the old adage, you get more flies with honey than with vinegar. That applies to your dealings with policymakers as well. Throughout all your communications, you should always be polite. Treating the staff poorly will not further your cause. Even though you may be frustrated with government, try not to treat every communication as an adversarial situation.

Tip #7: Be Patient

You should not expect an immediate response to your comments or concerns. In many cases, the issue may be one that the policymaker has not yet formed an opinion about. That said, it is perfectly appropriate to ask when you should call back to see if the official has taken a position. In fact, if you make it clear you're going to follow-up, they will be far more likely to focus on your "ask." See Chapter 12 for more ideas on following up.

Tip #8: Don't Make Ultimatums

The statement "if he/she doesn't agree with me on this issue, I won't vote for them" carries very little weight with a policymaker. For every person making that statement on one side of any issue, there is often another person making the same statement on the other side. Frankly, it is impossible to satisfy people who base their decisions on only one issue, and most officials won't bend over backwards to try.

Tip #9: Always Tell the Truth

This is a good rule for life as well as advocacy. Policymakers and their staff turn to outside individuals for advice and assistance on important policy issues all the time. They must feel that they can trust the individuals with whom they are dealing.

Tip #10: Don't Talk About the Campaign with Staff

Most staff get very nervous when people they are meeting with, from lobbyists to constituents, mention campaign-related issues. Some staffers may actually be offended. The laws against staff involvement in campaigns are very strict and wandering into any gray area can put both the official and the staff person at risk of violating federal or state election laws. Penalties range from fees to jail time. In particular, any suggestion that the staff person's help on a legislative issue may translate into a big campaign contribution is strictly forbidden. It is illegal, unethical and immoral for the policymakers to take specific actions in exchange for campaign contributions. Such a suggestion may, in fact, make a staff person avoid helping you because they are worried it would look bad for their boss.

★ Conclusion

Now that you know not to say things like "I was just dropping off a check at the campaign office, and that reminded me to come talk to you about a policy issue," you're ready to look at some specific options for getting your message across – from e-mails to phone calls to in-person meetings. In fact, you have a variety of options to have your message heard: all you have to do is choose what works for you and your audience!

A visit with your policymakers or their staff is a golden opportunity. You will be able to bend the ear of people who make decisions that could affect your business and way of life. You must think about how you will use that opportunity to be most effective. You must have a well-crafted message that is delivered in a timely and effective way. This chapter provides the following resources:

- Step-by-step process for planning an effective meeting.[1]
- Details on attending a meeting
- Leave-behind materials
- What NOT to say: The top ten list of things elected officials and their staff HATE to hear

★ Step-By-Step Process for Planning a Meeting

Step #1: Develop Your Message and Ask

Take a minute to review the previous chapters outlining the elements of effective messages, and be sure you have something important to say before requesting a meeting. A national or state level organization that works on your issues should be able to assist. You'll want to be ready to ask for something specific, explain why it's relevant to the official's district and demonstrate a personal connection to the

---

[1] Note that if you are attending a meeting as part of an organized lobby day, you may not have to worry about the first few steps in the process, such as deciding who or where to meet. With the assistance of your state or national organization, you may be able to leap in at the "requesting meetings" step. If you're lucky, your organization may be arranging the meetings for you, in which case you just have to worry about attending the meeting (which is intimidating enough!).

issues. Your ability to do so as part of your meeting request will capture more positive attention from the policymaker's office – and hopefully secure you a meeting time.

Step #2: Decide Who to Meet
Your previous work in identifying the audience most likely to be able to assist you with your particular issue will be invaluable in determining who you should meet with at which level of government. These audiences might include your U.S. House or Senate representatives, your State representatives or Governor's office or your local council members. Remember that for elected officials you must be able to establish a constituency relationship (i.e., you live, work or serve people in the elected official's district) in order to have the most success in arranging meetings.

Step #3: Decide Where to Meet
Many people immediately assume that all meetings with officials and their staff will take place in the state capitol or Washington, D.C. In fact, meetings can often be arranged in district offices as well, which can be easier on both your pocketbook and schedule. Following are issues to consider when deciding whether to meet in Washington, D.C., the state Capitol or back at home.

Meeting in Washington, D.C., with Members of the U.S. House or Senate or their Staff

When Will They Be in Town? District Work Periods
Both the House and Senate leadership, as well as your individual Members' office, can provide you with information about when Congress will be in session and when Members will be at home for a district or state work period (or "recess"). People often laugh at the term "district work period." Some think that a "district work period" is really a vacation. In truth, most Members go back to their districts or states and have even busier work schedules than they have in D.C. Yes, they do take vacations for maybe a couple weeks out of the year. But the rest of the time, they are working, usually seven days a week.

If you are going to be in Washington, D.C., and want a meeting with the member, it is especially important to ensure you are scheduling on a "voting day" (i.e., a day when votes are scheduled to be held). Members will almost always be in or around the office on days when votes are scheduled. The downside is that the member may be pulled away from the meeting for a vote.

Traditional District Work Periods
- Two weeks in mid-January
- One week around President's Day (February)
- Two weeks during March or early April for Easter
- One week for Memorial Day (end of May)
- One or two weeks around the Fourth of July
- The month of August
- Mid-October through December

Resource Tips

Check out links on the House and Senate home pages (www.house.gov under the Majority Whip link or www.senate.gov under the Legislative Activities link) for information on the schedule for the year, particularly when representatives and senators will be in D.C. and when they will be in their home districts. Note that the House and Senate do not take identical breaks.

Meeting in the State Capitol with State Representatives

Every state is different, so take some time to learn a little about the meeting culture for your particular state. Some state houses operate very similarly to the U.S. Congress, with the need to have a formal meeting scheduled. Others expect constituents to "stop by" or have specific hours set up on a daily or weekly basis to see any constituents who happen to be around. The key is to know what the "norm" is for your situation. Some questions you'll want to answer include:

- When will the legislature be in session? Like Congress, state legislatures have schedules but they vary from state to state. Take a look at the legislature's website to see when your legislature will be meeting.

- Do legislators expect you to set up a meeting? Usually a state level association should be able to provide you with this information. Alternatively, many state legislative websites include this kind of information. Or you can simply call the office and ask!

Meeting Locally

If you live in or near the district or state, consider setting up a meeting with your policymaker in his or her home office. Sometimes, it can be easier to get a meeting in the district than in Washington or the state Capitol, and it's much less expensive for you. It does not diminish your message in any way to have it delivered at home as opposed to at the Capitol. See Chapter 12, "Following Up" for ideas on setting up district meetings and site visits.

Step #4: Decide Who Should Attend

This step comes before actually requesting a meeting because your policymaker's office will likely want to know who will be in attendance at whatever meeting you request. As you think about who should attend the meeting, consider the following points:

- **Think About Who Will Help You Make Your Best Case** -- To be truly effective, you should have someone from the district or state at least present at the meeting, and preferably delivering the message. But there are other factors to consider as well, including who might be best suited to deliver your message to a particular policymaker. Your research on the policymaker's positions and background should help you make those decisions.

- **Limit the Size of Your Group** -- Sometimes there's strength in numbers. And sometimes, with large numbers, there's only chaos. Believe it or not, many officials' offices are tiny. For many visits, if you have more than three people with you, chances are you are going to have to meet in the hall because they literally do not have room for five or six people to sit together. One person who can deliver the message well sends a far more powerful message than a crowd that can't fit in the room does.

- **Do Not Set Up Several Individual Meetings to Deliver the Same Message** -- Once again, volume does not equal effectiveness. During annual meetings or at other times when several organizations with the same message are setting up meetings with policymaker's offices, it is always a good use of your time and your audience's time to try to coordinate your meetings. In fact, if you make it clear that you are trying to coordinate meetings, the policymaker's office may be willing to help by setting up a time and trying to secure one of the few meeting rooms that members can sign up for. Note, though, that these rooms are difficult to get, and almost always require two to three weeks' notice.

Step #5: Ask for a Meeting

Phew! You've decided what you want, who you want to meet with and who should attend the meeting. It's finally time to ask for a meeting. Following are some key points to keep in mind:

■ **Make a written request:** Before you call, send a fax, e-mail or letter (note, however, the restrictions on postal mail in Washington, DC) outlining when you would like to meet, who from your organization would participate in the meeting and what issues you would like to discuss. This written communication will almost always be sent to a scheduler or administrative assistant who can arrange the meeting.

If you aren't sure where to send this request, you can always call and ask, but do not expect to be able to make the request for the meeting over the phone. Although this may be possible in some state legislative situations, it is common practice in policymaker's offices to ask that all scheduling requests be made in writing. Your request is likely to be reviewed by several people -- the scheduler, the chief of staff, the legislative aide who works on your issues, and in some cases the representative or senator. A written request facilitates this process. Some people might ask why the scheduler couldn't simply write down the information during a phone discussion. The truth is schedulers live on the phone. If you are lucky enough to actually get through to them, there is absolutely no way they will have time to write down all your issues or the names of the people who would attend.

Take pains to make sure the request reflects your themes, your priorities, and, most importantly, your good reasons why the official should meet with you. This is best done in a short letter from you.

Also, be sure to let the scheduler know if you are a close friend of the official, or if the official has asked you to visit. Policymakers are rarely able to pass along to their assistants the names of all their close friends, so the scheduler may have absolutely no idea that you are one of them. And don't try to claim you are a close personal friend if you are not. Given the number of people your request will go through, including the policymaker, you will invariably be found out. In addition to being embarrassed, you are also not likely to get a meeting.

■ **Give the Scheduler Adequate Time to Plan:** After you've sent in your initial written request, place a call as early as a month but no later than two weeks before the date you would like a meeting to be sure your request has been received. Many offices do not like to schedule meetings too much in advance, because it is not always clear what the policymaker's vote or committee hearing schedule will be. For example, some hearings are scheduled with just one day's advance warning, meaning that the official may have to cancel any constituent meetings he/she had scheduled for that time.

■ **Don't "Drop By" (Unless That's the Custom)**: Although some state legislative organizations thrive on the "stop by" approach, the vast majority – and the U.S. Congress – really expect people to make appointments. Remember that staff and members can often have nine or ten meetings a day. Like you, these are busy, busy people, and if you don't call ahead to make an appointment, chances are they will be in a meeting, briefing, or hearing when you arrive. Policymakers and staff rarely ever have time to deal with unexpected, unscheduled visits. If you want to be sure to see someone to deliver your message, you need to call ahead of time.

✪ Attending the Meeting: What to Do and What to Expect

Any new meeting situation can be a little intimidating. The following tips will give you a better sense of what to expect for any meeting with a policymaker, as well as specific ideas for Washington, D.C.

What to Expect

When you walk in to the office, don't be surprised if it feels a little bit like a war zone. The telephones ring constantly, there are usually at least five TVs blaring coverage of the day's floor debate, and staff are running from one meeting to another. This is why it is so important for you to have thought about your message beforehand.

The person at the front desk (usually a staff assistant) will greet you. Let them know that you are there for a meeting and who the meeting is with (sometimes, your meeting will be with a staff person as opposed to a member). Then they will ask you to either have a seat in the usually VERY SMALL lobby or, if there's no space, ask you to wait outside. Don't be offended – there's just no room. The staff assistant will let the person you are meeting with know you are there and that person will come out to start the meeting.

Here's a good way to approach the meeting:

■ State who you are and make the district connection: For example, "My name is XX and I'm from the XX organization in the policymaker's district."

■ Explain why you're there: For example "We are hoping that the official will support H.R. 1234, which would do X, Y and Z." Or "we'd like the elected official to visit our facility in the district and gain more insights into how policy issues impact our business."

- Explain why it's important to you (hint: this is where your personal story comes in): "H.R. 1234 is important to me because it -- saves me money, makes me healthier, protects the environment" – whatever the case may be.

- As necessary / appropriate, refer to the leave behind materials (but please don't read them to the staff people).

- Ask if the official has taken a position on the issue (note that in many cases the answer will be "no.").

- Let them know that you're available to be a resource and that you'll follow-up to see if there are questions and/or if the official can support your position. Be sure to ask the best way to follow-up (phone / e-mail / meeting) and collect all contact information.

Overall Tips

- **Don't Arrive Too Early:** Sound odd? Yes. But officials' offices typically do not have large waiting areas. If you arrive well ahead of your planned meeting (say 20 minutes to half an hour) you may have to wait standing up, squished against a wall, or out in the hallway. It's best to arrive about five minutes before the scheduled meeting time.

- **Wear Comfortable Shoes!:** Part of the reason why legislatures are so intimidating is that many of them are made of marble – including the floors. They are hard to walk on for even a few minutes, let alone several hours. This is not the time for your Manolo pumps or, if you must wear them, put a pair of comfortable flats in your bag to change in to.

- **Be Flexible:** A number of things may happen that might seem unusual, like being asked to meet standing up in the hallway. Don't be insulted if the staff suggests a hall meeting. It simply means that either the office is too small for the number of people in your group or another meeting is already using the one available meeting space. Likewise, the official may be called away to vote during your meeting. You may have a meeting scheduled with the official, but due to last minute changes in the schedule, you may find you are meeting with a staff person. Just go with the flow!

- **If You Can't Attend, Coordinate with Your Group About Calling to Cancel:** It is surprising how many people feel that they don't need to call to cancel meetings that have been set up for them with policymakers' offices. If you aren't able to make a particular meeting, and you are the only one assigned to go, it is common courtesy to cancel. If there are other people scheduled to go, check with them to make sure that someone will be attending.

- **The Five-Minute Rule:** You must prepare to deliver your message powerfully and effectively in no more than five minutes. With the possible interference of votes, schedules running late, and last-minute emergencies, that may be all the time you'll have.

Specifics for Washington, D.C.

Since many organizations plan lobby day visits in Washington, D.C., it's appropriate to give some specific details for visiting members of Congress in our nation's capital.

Getting to Capitol Hill

- **Transportation:** Your organization may have arranged transportation to the Hill for your group. If not, or if you prefer to go on your own, know that the House-side offices are best reached by the Capitol South Metro Stop (on the blue and orange line), and the Senate-side offices are best reached by the Union Station Metro Stop (red line). You can also take a cab  and simply tell the cab driver the name of the office building you are going to (i.e., please take me to the Longworth House Office Building).

- **Security:** If you've been through an airport metal detector you will have no problem with getting through the security measures on Capitol Hill. They have a very similar system, although the lines are significantly shorter and you do not have to take your shoes off. Be sure to leave the guns, knives and incendiary devices at home!

The Capitol Hill Layout

- **Overview:** The Senate office buildings are Russell, Dirksen, and Hart, which are on the Senate side of the Capitol (the north side or to the left as you face the Capitol from the reflecting pool). The House office buildings are Cannon, Longworth, and Rayburn which are on the House side of the Capitol (the south side, or to the right as you face the Capitol from the reflecting pool). They are in the order noted above on each side. For example, Longworth is between Cannon and Rayburn and Dirksen is between Hart and Russell.

- **Getting In-between Buildings:** All of the office buildings and the Capitol itself are connected via underground tunnels. However, due to security reasons, you cannot walk between the House and Senate underground without a staff person. You can go between buildings on one side or the other (i.e., between House buildings and between Senate buildings). That said, if it is a nice day, I recommend against using the tunnels to go from building to building. Go outside instead. It is very easy to get lost underground.

  It takes about 20 minutes to walk from any of the Senate office buildings to any of the House office buildings. Note that it can also take 10 to 15 minutes to walk from Cannon to Rayburn (the two furthest House buildings) or from Hart to Russell (the two furthest Senate buildings) so give yourself time to get from meeting to meeting.

What to Leave Behind

In many cases, your national or state organization will provide leave behind materials. If you're developing your own, here are a few tips:

- **Save the Trees:** Limit what you leave behind: If you can boil your statement down to five minutes, you should be able to boil the essence of your materials down to one page. You may want to include a few pages of background material with your main message, but do not leave behind reams of paper. The better thing to do is to let staff know what kind of informational resources you have and make it clear that if they need any of the background material you would be happy to get it to them. You may even want to leave a "bibliography" indicating what materials you have and why they may be useful. In addition, if some of the information you would otherwise leave behind can be accessed on the web, leave behind a sheet with the web site address and a table of contents.

■ **Put Information in a File Folder:** Information that's in a file folder is far more likely to be stuck directly into a file drawer as opposed to the wastebasket. Simply put, three-ring binders, two-sided packets and the like may look pretty, but can become hard to deal with as they accumulate because they are more difficult to store. Imagine that you had six

meetings a day and every group gave you a packet or binder of information. Policymakers' offices do not have much storage space. In fact, most staffers have one, or at most two, file cabinets in which to store information. Rather than try to find somewhere to put the binder or packet, a staffer generally will toss everything except your business card, assuming that if they ever need to know anything they can call you. If you're lucky, they might remove some of the information from the packets and binders and store it in a manila file folder. So make it that much easier for them to keep your information by supplying it file-ready.

■ **A Word About Gifts:** Some visitors to policymaker's offices like to leave behind gifts to remind members and staff of the home state. It's definitely not required or expected, but if you plan to bring gifts, I recommend asking each individual office about their policy, perhaps at the time you set up an appointment. Due to recent public dismay over the

perception of gift-giving in D.C. and state capitols, many policymakers have adopted an "absolutely no gifts" rule.

★ What NOT to Say: The Top 10 Things Elected Officials and Their Staff HATE to Hear

Number 10: But I thought my appointment was with the Senator.
Never, ever indicate that you are disappointed to be meeting with a staff person. With legislatures, having a good relationship with a staff person can make or break your cause.

Number 9: Here's some reading material for you – our 300 page annual report.
When meeting with policymakers, try to limit your leave behind materials to one or two pages, and include details on where this information can be located on the web, if appropriate.   Offering the information in a file folder with your organization's name on the label will also help ensure that the materials are put in a file drawer, as opposed to the round file.

Number 8: How much of a campaign contribution did your boss get to vote against (or for) this bill?
Believe it or not, most staff have no idea who contributed to their boss' campaigns. Not only is this question insulting, but even if it were accurate, the staff person isn't likely to know.

Number 7: I assume you know all about HR 1234.
With thousands of bills being introduced during each legislative session , no staff person will be able to keep them all straight. Always provide information on the bill title, number and general provisions when communicating with a policymaker's office.

Number 6: No, I don't have an appointment, but I promise I'll only take ½ hour of your time.
If you weren't able to get an appointment, it's OK to stop by, drop off some materials and let them know of your interest in the issue. It is not OK to camp out in their doorway and demand that someone talk to you.

Number 5: No, I don't really need anything specific.
If you don't ask for something – a bill cosponsorship, a congressional record statement, a meeting in the district, whatever – some staff will wonder why you came by.   Updates on your issue are fine, so long as they are accompanied by a request.   That will ensure that someone in the office thinks about you and your request for longer than 5 minutes.

Number 4: What you're telling me can't be right. I heard Jon Stewart on the Daily Show say otherwise.
If you watch The Daily Show on the Comedy Channel, you know it's funny. But the legislative reports are not always 100% accurate. Whether it's the Comedy Channel or the Internet, be sure you're basing your message on accurate information.

Number 3: We have 10 (or more) people in our group.
Offices are tiny. If you have more than 5 people in your group, you'll be standing out in the hallway. Plus, having so many people talking at once can dilute the impact of your message. Try to limit your group to no more than 5. If you do have a large group, assign a few people (specifically constituents) the responsibility of delivering the message.

Number 2: What do you mean we have to stand in the hall?
See number 3. A request to meet in the hallway is simply an indication of space limitations. Nothing else.

Number 1: No, I don't represent anyone from your district or committee interest. I just thought you'd be interested in what I have to say.
Elected officials are elected to represent their constituents. Period. If you are not their constituent or you are not connected to their constituents, you are not relevant to them. Some members do rise to higher positions, but that just means they represent the interest of other members, not the entire nation. Your time is always best spent working with your own elected official and turning them into an advocate for your cause.

★ Conclusion
A meeting with a policymaker or staff person is one of the most effective ways to influence a policy outcome. Unfortunately, they can also be one of the fastest ways to either waste time or, worse, alienate those whose help you really need -- but not for you, brave reader. Armed with the information in this chapter you're ready to use this powerful tool to achieve your own issue goals!

In 2004, the U.S. Congress received over 200 million e-mails, four times more than in 1995. By the end of 2008, that number is expected to be close to 500 million. Although many citizens have switched to e-mail as their main form of written communication, postal mail is also still popular, with offices receiving over 20 million letters a year.

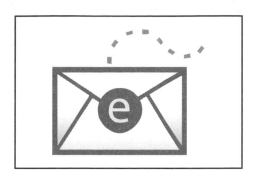

The bad news is that the vast majority of these communications are nowhere near as effective as they should be. The good news is that your communications will stand out – and all because you're reading this book.

To help ensure that your written correspondence, whether sent by postal mail, e-mail, fax or carrier pigeon, is as effective as possible, this chapter will outline several key points specific to written communications, including:

- Which written form is best?
- Applying overall message rules to written correspondence
- Three tips for effective written communications
- A template for written communications

★ Which Written Form Is Best?

There are a lot of myths and misperceptions about written communications. In fact, you may have heard that "e-mail doesn't work" or "personal handwritten notes are always best."

In general, though, what really matters is the message. A thoughtful, personal relevant e-mail will have far more influence than an angry, rambling handwritten letter from someone that is in no way relevant to an official. It's more important to focus on **what** you're saying than **how** you say it. A well-

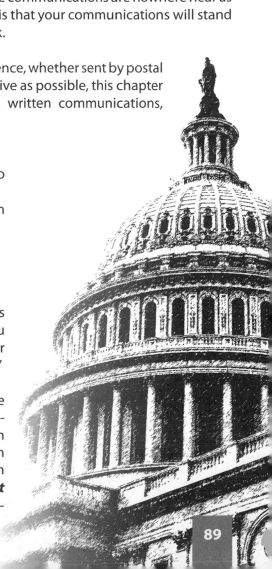

crafted and thoughtful message delivered in any one of these ways will be given equal attention.

There is one important caveat to this general advice. Unfortunately, security measures were dramatically increased in Washington, D.C., in the wake of Anthrax mailings to the U.S. House and Senate. As a result, all postal mail must endure a radiation process which takes time and weakens the integrity of the paper. In short, radiated mail comes out of the process late and not looking very good. Given this situation, e-mails and faxes may be a better way to reach the Washington, D.C., staff. As an alternative, you can consider sending letters or packages that must go through the postal mail to the official's district office.

✪ Applying Overall Message Rules to Written Correspondence

So if it's the message that matters, how can you ensure that your written correspondence hits the right notes? Earlier chapters discussed, at length, several important concepts that apply to all communications. Following is a review of those concepts and how they apply to written correspondence. In short, your written messages should be:

■ **Relevant:** You'll need to demonstrate your relevance to the policymaker with whom you're communicating. For elected officials, that means you'll need to either have an in-district address or demonstrate some other level of connection, such as having employees in their district or state, for example. For regulators, you should be able to show a certain level of expertise on policy issues as well as a direct connection to the issues being addressed by the agency. See Chapter 7 for more information on establishing relevancy.

■ **Thoughtful:** The key to being effective in your written communications is ensuring that someone on staff actually thinks about what you have to say. Your "voice" must be heard above the cacophony of voices represented by the flood of postcards, letters, e-mails, and faxes that pour into policymakers' offices every day. By

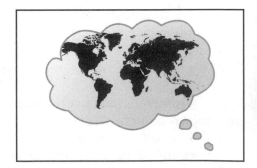

far, the most compelling and effective letters combine a thoughtful approach to policy issues with a careful explanation of why it's important to the author personally. In most offices, it is these letters that the official actually sees.

Example

During the impeachment hearings and trial of President Clinton, the office I was working in received thousands of communications on the subject. The representative was spending a great deal of time thinking about what course of action he should take. Reviewing the thoughtful comments on both sides of the issue from our constituents really helped. The staff culled the most thoughtful written communications and passed them along to the congressman. Many of these, representing both sides of the issue, were posted on our website so that others could review them and consider the arguments.

Because so few people take the time to craft thoughtful, personal letters, doing so almost guarantees that you'll capture the interest and attention of someone in the office.

Example

One Member of Congress I worked for asked to see three to four of the most thoughtful and well-argued constituent letters per week, regardless of the topic or whether we agreed with the writer. Within two weeks of trying to comply with this request, I realized that we received, at most, one or two thoughtful letters a week. The vast majority of the correspondence consisted of form letters, postcards, and personal letters full of inappropriate language and personal slurs. As a result, the few thought-provoking letters received considerable attention from the member.

Personal: Remember the advice in Chapter 6 about volume not necessarily equaling effectiveness? This advice applies to written communications as well, specifically to coordinated postcard, petition, blast fax, and e-mail campaigns. The theory behind these campaigns is that a high volume of mail on a particular topic will get noticed and sway opinion. In reality, one thoughtful, well-argued letter can have more impact than 100 postcards or petition signatures. Why?

Because policymakers and their staff recognize the time and energy spent writing the thoughtful letter. It sends a signal that the constituent really cares about the issue -- and perhaps cares even more than the constituents who simply signed their names to a postcard do.

Example

In one of the congressional offices I worked in, we had received a number of form letters in support of legislation to limit the use of lost, stolen, or homeless pets for research. People had simply signed postcards they received from their local animal shelter. I sensed that people who sent the postcards really wanted us to do more than be aware of the legislation and vote for it if it ever came to a vote (which was highly unlikely). This was a reasonable request, but the postcards did not inspire me to think more about the issue or to consider whether my boss should cosponsor the bill. Then I ran across a letter from a constituent whose pet had been stolen from his backyard and who had discovered that a number of pets had been stolen from that neighborhood and sold to a research facility. The constituent never found out what happened to the family's pet. That letter made a bigger impression on me then all the postcards put together. It inspired me to find time to look into the bill and ultimately recommended that my boss sign on as a cosponsor.

Brief: Do your best to keep the written communication to one page or, even better, one "screen" for e-mails. With so many communications to review and respond to, officials and their staff appreciate your efforts to get to the point – quickly.

✪ Three Tips for Written Communications

In addition to the overall message rules noted above, there are a few additional approaches to consider that apply specifically to written communications. If you incorporate all these ideas, your correspondence will stand out – in a positive way!

Ask for a Response: Given the limited time and budgets in a policymaker's office, priority will always be given to letters that require an answer. Asking for a response means someone on the staff has to think about what you've said and, in some way, address your concerns or comments. If you make it impossible for the office to respond (by not including your address, for example) you virtually assure that no one will think about what you had to say.

Example

A congressional office I worked in received a few hundred postcards as part of a coordinated campaign against privatization of social security. The printed return address on the postcards included the city and state only, making it impossible for us to respond, or even know whether the writers were constituents. We simply threw the postcards away and devoted our resources to responding to people who had written personal letters about the issue.

■ **Confine Letters to One Subject:** If you have strong views on a number of topics you want to bring up with policymakers, it may be more effective to write individual letters for each topic. This is especially true if the subject areas are wide-reaching. By confining your written communications to discrete subjects, you will likely receive a response much more quickly because your letter won't need to be reviewed by as many staff people before a response can be drafted.

■ **Double Check Congressional Addresses and Phone Numbers:** Policymakers change office locations often and will sometimes change their fax numbers and/or e-mail addresses. Unfortunately, not everyone takes the time to forward misdirected mail, faxes, and e-mails to the appropriate office. There's nothing more frustrating than waiting for a response only to find your correspondence was never received.

★ Template for Written Communications

Written communications arriving at a public official's office are typically routed through staff members with only a select few actually reaching the officeholder. To be most successful, your written communication should be persuasive and to the point. The most effective format is a regular, typed business communication no longer than one or two pages (or for e-mails one or two screens). State your message clearly at the start of the communication and then provide details of your personal story. Consider utilizing the following format to develop a truly winning written communication.

First Paragraph

- Identify yourself as a constituent or someone that represents a constituent or local interest.
- Connect the issue to something the policymaker cares about, if possible.
- Identify the reason for writing and the issue(s) you wish to address. Be sure to make the "ask" early.
- Highlight any relevant expertise on that issue.
- Mention anything relevant (and factual) about the number of other people in the district or state concerned about the issue.

Second Paragraph

- State your views on the issue in your own words.
- Include a statement about the impact specific state or federal policies have on you or your business.

Third Paragraph

- Clearly state what you would like the official to do (i.e., make the "ask").

Closing Paragraph

- Thank the official for his or her attention to this matter and offer to be available for any questions.

In some cases, it may make sense to call opinion leaders. This is especially true for very short term, immediate asks, such as asking an official to vote yes or no on a certain policy issue. Calling a policymaker leaves a much more personal and direct impression than a written communication. This chapter offers a few tips to make sure the impression you're leaving is a positive one, specifically:

- Adapting your message to a phone call
- Deciding who to call
- Developing your talking points
- Managing questions
- Asking for a response

✪ Adapting Your Message for a Phone Call

Chapter 7 covered the details of developing an effective message. The core principles of ensuring that your message is relevant, personal, specific and brief apply to phone calls as well. A phone communication works particularly well for certain circumstances, such as:

- Short and urgent messages, such as "vote yes" or "vote no" on a bill that is being considered in the near future
- Direct communications with staff people with whom you've developed a relationship
- Following up on previous communications with the office (such as e-mails or meetings)
- Setting up meetings with staff or following up on meeting requests with members
- Press or media inquiries

Phone communications generally aren't a good way to introduce a new idea, although if this is your only option you should certainly use it.

★ Deciding Who to Call

Who you call in the office (or, for that matter, which office you call), will depend in large part on what you're asking for. Some messages can be left with the person answering the phone, where others might require a more substantive conversation with the relevant staff person. Review the following circumstances to help you determine who it would be most appropriate for you to call:

- **Short message registering your position on a specific vote or bill:** If your goal is to relay your opinion about how a policymaker should vote on a particular issue, you can feel comfortable calling and leaving that message with the person who answers the phone. For these types of communications, you can call either the state capitol (for messages to state legislators), the U.S. Capitol in Washington D.C. (for messages to the U.S. Congress) office or the local office of either legislature to avoid the toll charges. Each of these offices are used to receiving phone calls from constituents and have processes in place to manage and categorize the opinions expressed.

- **Policy discussions:** If you want to have a substantive discussion about a particular policy issue, you should call and ask for the staff person who handles that issue. If you would like to chat with them for longer than 15 minutes, ask if you can set up a phone appointment – the staff greatly appreciate your recognition of their busy schedules. To save toll charges, you might want to start with the district or state staff person, although you may eventually be referred to the state capitol or Washington, D.C. staff.

- **Scheduling requests for staff:** In most offices with staff, the staff people manage their own schedules. If you would like to have them visit a facility or meet with you while you're in the state capitol or D.C., you should call the staff directly to request the meeting.

- **Scheduling requests for officials:** Chapter 9 covered the process of requesting a meeting with officials. Recall that most initial requests should be made in writing. About a week after the initial request has been sent in, it may make sense to call the office to follow-up. These requests should be directed to the scheduler or administrative aide.

- **Press or Media Inquiries:** If you are approaching an elected official in a media capacity (i.e., to ask an elected official to write an article for your newsletter), it may be appropriate to ask for the press person. Many state legislators and all Members of the U.S. Congress have folks that fit this description.

★ Developing Your Talking Points

When calling about a particular issue, always be ready to provide basic information, such as a bill number and title, if you are asking the official to support a specific bill.

If you are calling as part of a coordinated campaign, be sure to carefully review the organization's talking points but also be prepared to explain your position in your own words. It is always abundantly clear to staff when constituents call as part of a coordinated campaign and aren't really sure what they're talking about. Make sure the message you are delivering is your own, not anyone else's.

Example
During a debate on an amendment to an appropriation bill, a national interest group started calling people in our district to discuss the amendment and why that interest group thought the representative should support it. Once the constituent agreed with the group's position, they were immediately transferred to our office so they could express their opinion, although most of the time they had no idea what they were talking about. The conversations would go something like this:

Interest group to constituent: "There is an amendment to the interior appropriation bill to protect your drinking water from contamination. Do you agree that Representative So-and-So should support it?"

Constituent: "Umm, yeah, I guess so"

Interest group: "Great, I'm connecting you to that office. Please tell them the same thing."

Congressional office: "Good Morning, Representative So-and-So's office."

Constituent to congressional office: "Hi, I'm calling to let you know that I think the congressman should vote to keep our drinking water clean."

Congressional office: "Is there a particular proposal you wanted him to support?"

> **Constituent:** "I heard there was something that was maybe going to be voted on in some bill about the interior."
>
> **Congressional office:** "There are 50 amendments to the bill we're considering today. Do you know which one it is or who's offering it?"
>
> **Constituent:** "I'm not really sure. I think it has something to do with drinking water."
>
> **Congressional office:** "There are five different amendments dealing in some way with drinking water. Can you give us some idea of which one you're supporting?"

And so on. While it's always appropriate to be unsure of legislative details (after all, the legislative process is often long and convoluted), be sure that you're familiar enough with the issue you're calling about to answer basic questions. If you're going to be strongly supportive of a particular idea, be sure you know why. Likewise, be sure you really should be outraged before you call about something all in a huff.

★ Managing Questions

When talking on the phone with officials or their staff, you may find yourself confronted with a question you don't know the answer to. The best response is a simple "I don't know, but I'll get back to you," – and then get back to them! Policymakers ask questions for several reasons. For example, they might want to better understand policy matters, or they may hope to get a sense of your expertise on the matter as well as your ability and willingness to get questions answered in the future.

★ Always Ask for a Response

As with written communications, the key to effective communication by phone is ensuring that someone actually thinks about what you have to say. Some offices tally phone messages from people seeking to "express their opinion" on a topic, but it's not always the best way to ensure that your message is heard and carefully considered.

Asking for a response serves a variety of purposes. First, you are demonstrating that you care enough about the issue to want to know more. Second, you are forcing someone in the office to put enough thought into the issue to draft a letter from the policymaker about the topic. Finally, officials generally prefer to reflect the opinions and views of their constituents. If a policymaker has enough people calling or writing on a particular issue (and all these people want to know what the policymaker is going to do), he or she might be more inclined to follow the course proposed. That way, the written response is more likely to be of the "I agree with you 100 percent" variety, instead of the "I'm afraid we'll have to disagree" type.

A Sample Phone Script

Congressional office: Hello, Senator so-and-so's office.

Constituent: Hello. My name is Mary Jones and I am a constituent. I am calling to express my support of legislation that the Senator will be voting on today.

Congressional office: I'd be happy to relay your views to the Senator. What vote are you calling about?

Constituent: I'm calling about an amendment to the Interior Appropriation bill that would increase the amount of funding available to local communities to purchase and preserve land in watershed areas. It is my understanding that this proposal will increase the purity of our drinking water by reducing the potential for pollution due to run-off an industrial waste. This is important to me because our community has had problems in the past with particulat matter in our drinking water. I would like to feel comfortable in giving tap water to my two children and I think this legislation would help.

Congressional office: Thank you, I will pass that message along.

Constituent: Thank you. Could you please send me a response indicating how the Senator voted? My address is: [   ]

12 | FOLLOWING UP

Even if you deliver the perfect message and make a compelling ask, whether it's in a meeting, on the phone or in a written communication, you should be prepared to follow-up on your request. This is especially true when you've attended a lobby day or other type of meeting with an elected official or their staff. There is simply no way that you will be able to relay everything you know about an issue in your initial brief communication. Plus, the officials you're talking to will likely have questions about the issues you raise that you will need to answer. This is why follow-up is so essential.

In fact, in most cases, policymakers won't be able to give you an answer right away on your "ask." They may response in a vaguely positive way, saying something like "that's sounds interesting" or "I'd like to learn more." While it's tempting to think that they are stalling, the truth is much less sinister. In fact, officials often wait to make a decision about the requests that come from constituents for one of three reasons:

- The official simply forgot about the request -- with dozens of requests a day, this happens often
- The elected official hasn't had time to form an opinion on your question
- The elected official is waiting to see how much you really want what you're asking for

All three of these situations can be resolved through effective follow-up. You can remind them about your request, you can gently prod them to make a decision, and you can demonstrate your commitment to the cause!

This chapter offers insights into how you can be most effective in your follow-up, as well as three specific follow-up techniques that will put you on the path to advocacy success.

★ Tips for Effective Follow-Up

The following tips for effectively following up with your policymakers will help you build long-term relationships with them that will serve the effective advocate well when seeking to create lasting change. And as the following ideas show, the phrase "long-term relationship" does not have to equal "big-time campaign contributions".

- **Ask Again!** The number one thing any advocate can do to let an official or staff person know they are serious about the "ask" is to ask again – and keep asking, politely but persistently, until they get an answer. If you get an answer you don't like, ask a different question! Perhaps a policymaker can't support you right now on a legislative matter, but he or she may be willing to take some time to do a site visit or make a public statement about his or her views.

- **Say "Thank You":** Even if you didn't get exactly what you wanted out of the meeting, it's appropriate to thank the official or staff person for taking the time to meet with you. Most people are in the office to ask for something or express dissatisfaction – those who take a few minutes to say "thank you" really stand out! You can do this by dropping off a handwritten note, sending an e-mail or sending a fax.

- **Use the Preferred Method of Communication:** Like all people, policymakers and staff have individual communication styles. Some love to touch base by phone, others prefer e-mail. Some like to take five minutes to meet face-to-face. Most staff will really appreciate it (and think positively about you and your efforts) if you ask them whether it's best to update them via phone, fax, e-mail, or in a meeting. And then, of course, use that method, NOT the one you prefer.

- **Work with Others:** If you are making your ask in conjunction with a national or state organization, work closely with them on ideas for "tweaking" your ask to make it more palatable to your specific policymakers, or to identify very specific and appropriate options for follow-up. Often, the government relations staff for the organization will have great ideas for setting up community meetings, putting together statements or making plans for future lobby events.

- **Become An Ongoing Resource:** Because they must, by necessity, be generalists, most policymakers and their staff usually are not experts on all issues. Therefore, they are always turning to trusted outside experts when legislation that impacts their constituents is on the table. Let the staff know if you have done research on specific areas of your issues. Knowing that there's someone in the district who really understands the needs of those groups can be very helpful, because they'll know who to call to get the details they need to make an informed decision.

■ **Make sure they receive your newsletters:** Add the official's local, state, and national offices (where appropriate) to your newsletter list, and be sure to address the materials to a particular staff person. In addition to the legislative staff, the press secretary is likely to be interested. But be aware that given the staff's crushing work and mail load, there is no guarantee the information will be read. Your goal in providing this material is to simply "stay on the radar screen."

■ **Assemble a townhall panel:** Offer to put together a panel of experts in your field for a district-based townhall meeting. Many policymakers have these meetings every few months to highlight important concerns or receive feedback from constituents. See the information below about coordinating or attending townhall meetings

■ **Use new technologies, including social networks and "Web 2.0" approaches to stay in touch:** Long considered a tool of members of the youngish crowd to communicate with others of the youngish crowd in their incomprehensible language, social networks, instant messaging tools and blogs can play an important role in connecting advocates with policymakers in a meaningful way. Consider following-up through one of the following approaches:

● "Friend" your elected officials on Facebook: Being listed as a supporter may gain you early access to important policy information. At a minimum, the official or a relevant staff person may notice and appreciate your support!

● Use LinkedIn to find members of your network that are currently or have previously been affiliated with policymakers. In establishing a profile on this site, you can search for those that may have previously worked with elected officials. Who knows? Your elected official may be on the site and you can connect with him or her directly.

- Subscribe to your policymaker's blogs and comment (positively, please) on entries related to your issues. Many policymakers maintain a blog as a means of communicating with constituents on a more frequent basis than a quarterly newsletter allows. In subscribing and occassionally commenting, you send the message that you care enough about the issues to follow the elected official's actions.

- Post photos or videos from any meetings on YouTube or Flickr: Photo and video-sharing sites give you the ability to post photos from any meetings you've attended, whether a session at the state capitol or a district site visit. Be sure to send the link to policymakers to keep them apprised. In general, they appreciate the opportunity to advertise the fact that they have been meeting with constituents. Your photos of the event help them achieve that goal.

- Subscribe to your policymaker's Twitter feed – or start your own!: Twitter, a "micro-blogging" site, offers users the ability to send very short messages (called "tweets") to anyone choosing to subscribe. Some policymakers use this site to post brief notices about meetings, new resources and new perspectives on policy issues. Explore the site as an option not only for connecting with policymakers, but to share your own views.

▪ **Keep the momentum rolling...** Ask for occasional meetings, statements, and letters related to important milestones with your programs. Don't just inform your elected officials that a program is celebrating its 10th anniversary; ask them to submit a congratulatory statement for the Congressional Record. Similarly, don't just let the office know that you've applied for an important grant; ask for and prepare a draft letter of support. Instead of informing your representatives that you're adding a wing to your facility, ask them to attend the groundbreaking ceremony[1].

▪ **...without being a pest:** Of course, there's a difference between making relevant contact every few months and calling up every other day just to chat. While it's important to stay on their radar screen, it's imperative NOT TO BE A PEST. The last thing you want is to be the "oh, no, not him again" person. You should limit your requests to a few per year. Keep your communications short and purposeful and you'll be looked at as a resource instead of a nuisance. Be open to direct and indirect feedback from the staff as to whether your communications are welcome or becoming burdensome.

---

[1] See the next section on ideas for putting these types of follow-up events together.

✪ Three Follow-Up Techniques That Work

While there are certainly many ways to build long term relationships with policymakers, three key techniques stand out as truly effective means to ensure that officials and their staff stay connected to and up-to-date on your issues. These three important follow-up techniques are:

- Site Visits
- Statements / Letters of Support
- Attending or Coordinating Townhall Meetings

We'll look at each in more detail.

✪ Site Visits

Chapter 9 on Effective Meetings introduced the idea of "site visits" or "district visits." We'll delve in to a little more detail below.

What is a Site Visit?
A "site visit" is an in-person visit by a policymaker or staff to a facility, office or location in the district or state. These visits are invaluable to helping officials understand the impact of proposed policies on individuals and businesses in their district.

When's the best time to schedule a visit?
Most policymakers spend a considerable amount of time "at home" during what's known as "district work periods" or "recess." Calendars for the U.S. Congress are available through the House and Senate websites at www.house.gov and www.senate.gov. You can usually find a legislative calendar for the state legislature on the state legislative website.

Do only officials do site visits?
Actually, it can be very effective to ask a staff person to do a visit before you ask his or her boss. That way, assuming you make the visit as interesting as possible, you can turn the staff person into an advocate for future visits. Officials sometimes make decisions about where they might spend their time based on a positive experience their staff person may have had. In addition, the staff are very influential in terms of the policy decisions made in the office – getting them up to speed is always a good idea.

How do I set up a site visit?
Following is a step-by-step process for setting up a winning site visit.

- Figure Out What you Want to Show: Be sure to consider how what you're showing a policymaker connects to the issue you want them to think about. For example, if you are trying to make the case for why you need more funding for a program, it's a good idea to show them the need, as well as how you have usefully (and frugally) spent money in the past.

- Decide Who to Invite: There are a number of factors involved in this decision. Is this a visit for staff or officials or a combination? We strongly recommend that you do not ignore the staff. Likewise, be cognizant of the political situation in your community. You want to be sure to invite the right local officials and not step on any toes.

- Draft the Invitation: Your one-page letter of invitation should be directed to the official's scheduler or executive assistant, usually in the district office. Call about one week after sending the first request to ensure it has been received and to answer any questions.

- Dealing with Logistics: For any site visit you will need to worry about pretty much everything, including:

  - Transportation: How will the officials get to and from the event?
  - Time: How much time can the official commit to the event? Do not try to cram too much into a short visit. Make sure you hit the highlights.
  - Food: If this visit is going to occur during a regular mealtime, you should consider setting up a discussion over an informal buffet or box lunch.
  - Weather: Obviously, you can't control the weather, but you can be prepared for all possibilities. Make sure you have enough umbrellas, bug spray, or whatever you'll need to make the visit pleasant for everyone.

- Making the Case: Think carefully about who you want from your program to help you make the case, while keeping the total number of people actively participating to no more than five. Following are some types to consider:

  - Practitioners: Officials enjoy speaking with the people who perform the day-to-day tasks of the program or project.
  - Beneficiaries: "Real people" who already benefit from your work (or will in the future) and can speak with conviction and enthusiasm about your services will always impress visitors.

- Funders/Supporters: Having those who have invested in your good works or who are leaders in the community present at the visit demonstrates support you enjoy.

■ Recording The Event & When To Bring In The Media: You want to be sure to capture this auspicious occasion. Some aspects to consider include:

- Photographer: Consider hiring a photographer or have someone on your staff designated to take pictures for use in a newsletter or on a website.
- Note taker: Although you don't want someone writing down every word out of the official's mouth, do assign someone the task of preparing a written report after the visit.
- Consider inviting the media - but only after warning the official!

Sketch Out a Plan for a Visit

Take a few minutes to sketch out some ideas:

What Will You Show?: _____

_____

_____

Who Will You Invite? _____

_____

_____

What is Your Timeline for Issuing the Invitation? Who Will You Write To and How Will You Follow-Up? _____

_____

_____

Are There Logistical Issues You Need to Deal With? If so, What? _____

_____

_____

Who Will Help You Make the Case? _____

_____

_____

What Are Your Plans for Recording the Event? _____

_____

_____

★ Putting Together a Statement / Letter of Support

Policymakers often make public statements, either verbally, through speeches, or in written communications. These might include a letter of support for a grant request, a public statement in support of a particular position during a debate or a statement that is submitted "for the record." Following are some approaches to consider, depending on your needs and audience.

Letter of Support for a Grant Request

While policymakers cannot guarantee a grant request or government action in your favor, they can often express support for your request with the organization making the grant. This is particularly useful for grants available from government entities, which may be more likely to take the letter of support seriously, especially since the official sending the letter might have something to say about the governmental entity's budget! To avoid the appearance of favoritism, these letters generally won't be too overt. They might say something like, "I hope you will give this grant request every consideration," as opposed to "Please approve this grant request."

Federal Level Congressional Record Statement

Members of Congress have the ability to submit statements about pretty much anything under the sun in the "Extension of Remarks" section of the Congressional Record. You can see samples at http://thomas.loc.gov/r109/r109.html. Click on the "extension of remarks" links under the various dates. As you'll see, many of these statements are about people, places or events in various Congressional districts. It's best to have something drafted before you ask the office if they'd be willing to submit. Following is a good outline for a statement.

Opening paragraph: I would like to take this opportunity to congratulate [blank] on [blank]. For example, "I would like to take this opportunity to congratulate company X on its 50 year anniversary," or "I would like to take this opportunity to congratulate organization Y on its successful fundraising effort."

Second paragraph: Provide details on the company / organization / person / situation being discussed. Be sure to include how it relates to the Congressperson's district.

Third paragraph: If there was anything the Congressperson did to help make the event possible, be sure to mention that. For example, "I was proud to write a letter in support of the grant that made this program possible."

Fourth paragraph / closing: Reiterate the opening and the connection to the district.

State Level Public Statement of Support

Some state legislatures or governor's offices have a proclamation process or similar practice, whereby officials can express support for a particular issue, group or undertaking. They may agree to issue statements, award plaques or you may even be able to get the state to designate a certain month as [fill-in-your-issue-here] month! While these types of public expressions of support should not be the end goal of all your advocacy efforts, they can serve to generate enthusiasm and public expressions of interest in your cause. Explore the options for your state by reviewing your state's legislative and gubernatorial sites. A state-level organization may also be able to assist you with this approach.

⭐ Attending a Townhall Meeting

One of the most effective ways to gain the attention of policymakers and their staff is to attend a townhall or community meeting. Officials arrange these meetings to hear from people in their districts and states. They generally occur during district work periods or when the legislature is out of session. You can find out the schedule for your own officials by calling their office or checking their website. Many officials send notices to any constituents on their e-mail lists as well.

What happens during a townhall meeting? Although the format varies from state to state and Member to Member, usually, the official makes some opening remarks and introduces his or her staff. There may be local leaders in attendance as well who wish to make remarks. Then, the floor is opened up to comments from the audience.

Before you attend a townhall meeting, take a moment to learn a little about the official hosting the event. Review Chapter 6 on what you should know about your officials before communicating with them. And, as always, be sure to work with your national or state level organization, as appropriate, to guarantee that you are delivering the right message.

⭐ Conclusion

Whether you decide to set up a meeting in the district, propose a statement for the Congressional Record, or simply subscribe to an elected official's blog and post the occassional comment, the most important thing to remember about follow-up is, simply to do it! Most advocates ask elected officials to do something once and then are disappointed when the official doesn't immediately send a personalized communication indicating his or her support of their position.

If you think about it, though, is this a reasonable perspective? Remember that many policy-related asks, such as supporting funding for a project, choosing to approve the establishment of a program or deciding to side with one powerful interest over another incurs costs for the policymaker, These costs may be political support, time, funding for a campaign or even the ability to move forward on an issue of personal importance to the policymaker.

As frustrating as it can sometimes be, we should be pleased that elected officials take some time to deliberate carefully on the policy asks with which they are presented. Those advocates that take the time to follow-up – to demonstrate their ongoing commitment not only to the policy issue at hand, but to a long-term and genuine relationship with the official – will have far more success than those who ask once and then never ask again.

⭐ A Word of Caution – and a Ray of Hope

Advocates that carefully follow all the directions in this book by developing personalized, relevant, specific communications, building long-term relationships, and following-up on all requests will almost certainly receive more attention to their issues than those who don't. That said, these techniques cannot always guarantee that an elected official will agree with you 100% of the time (or ever, for that matter).

Reaching agreement is far more likely utilizing these techniques than not, but it is rarely a given.

There is one thing that always works in advocacy, however. That magic solution is persistence. OK, it's a pretty terrible silver bullet, but it works. As Calvin Coolidge said:

"Nothing in the world can take the place of Persistence. Talent will not; nothing is more common than unsuccessful men with talent. Genius will not; unrewarded genius is almost a proverb. Education will not; the world is full of educated derelicts. Persistence and Determination alone are omnipotent. The slogan "Press On", has solved and will always solve the problems of the human race."

Or, for the more Zen-oriented:

"Persistence can grind an iron beam down in to a needle."

Sure, it takes a long time, and it's not very enjoyable for the iron beam, but it works. You may need to maintain your commitment to your ultimate goal for years, celebrating small victories along the way. In some cases, you may need to shift your priorities, strategies and tactics to match your ultimate goal with the current policy environment. You may even need to redefine success in the short term. But be assured, whether it's securing a certain tax break for your business, establishing environmental protection programs or seeing an African-American as President of the United States, with enough genuine enthusiasm for your cause and the assistance of others, you'll get there. After all, that's what the democratic process is all about!

ABOUT THE AUTHOR

Stephanie D. Vance

With 20 years of experience in Washington, D.C., Stephanie Vance, known nationally and internationally as the Advocacy Guru, knows the insider's secrets to influencing government. She has worked at a prominent D.C. law firm, as a lobbyist for National Public Radio and as a Congressional aide, holding positions as Legislative Director and Staff Director for three different members of Congress. She is the author of Government by the People: How to Communicate with Congress and the fabjob.com guide Get a Job on Capitol Hill.

Stephanie's work stems from a deep and abiding belief that the U.S. system of government is effective only when citizens are active and well-informed participants. She helps citizens across the country take action through her speeches and training sessions for groups both small and large, including nationally recognized organizations like the American Library Association and the Humane Society of the United States. Her message has been heard by tens of thousands of advocates across the country and around the world many of whom are making the world a better place (at least in their view) through the application of her advice.

Ms. Vance holds a Bachelor's Degree in Political Science as well as two Master's degrees, one in Legislative Affairs from George Washington University and the other in Liberal Studies from Georgetown University (this is not the study of how to be a liberal). A member of the National Speakers Association, she recently earned the NSA's prestigious Certified Speaking Professional designation. She is also a member of the American Society of Association Executives, Women in Government Relations and is mentioned in Who's Who in American Women.